Lewis Davies was born in Penrhiwtyn in 1967.
He has won a number of awards for his writing.

Parthian
The Old Surgery
Napier Street
Aberteifi
SA43 1ED
www.parthianbooks.co.uk

First published in 1993, reprinted 1996, 1999, 2003
©Lewis Davies
All Rights Reserved
ISBN 0-9521558-0-x
Edited by Ravi Pawar

Typeset in Georgia by JW
Cover design John Tomlinson
Photograph from photolibrarywales.com
With thanks to Steve John

Printed and bound by Dinefwr Press, Llandybïe

Parthian is an independent publisher that works with the
support of the Welsh Books Council and the Arts Council of
Wales.

Work, Sex and Rugby

Lewis Davies

By the same author

For 53, Colum Road

Who knows or dares to dream
Simon Day

The beams of the headlights chipped fleetingly at the blackness. Twisting across the contours before returning to the slim farm road hemmed in by tight stone walls; standing dry and sombre in the black and the wet of the mountain.

Lewis drove automatically. He'd been around the road so many times: first as a kid on a bike; then while still under age in a mini estate, bought cheaply with a friend and now and recently with any girl who would believe him.

'How much further does this road go on for?' the girl asked him.

'Not much further now, then we'll be turning back,' Lewis replied.

He continued driving, changing down as the car struggled to take the bend which had seen the end of the mini estate.

'I don't like it up here, I can't see anything.'

'It'll be alright; you'll be able to see down the valley soon,' assured Lewis.

'Can we go back, please, Lewis?'

'Don't worry, the road comes out in the village.'

The girl did not reply but he could feel the atmosphere of cordial sex he had spent the whole evening developing gently slip away into the mist swallowing the hollows. He had been with Louise on the odd Saturday night in the Cherub but this was the first time he had taken her out mid-week. It had not been a success. Two drinks in a sufficiently obscure pub had left him in desperate need of the cinema; he had watched the film. Weekdays were not useful for occasional women. Weekdays meant relationships and commitments. He had enough commitments. But despite the evening, the expensive drinks, the pub that looked like the inside of a bingo hall and the predictable film, here he was driving Louise around the mountain: it was not over yet. He slowed the car.

'What are we stopping for?'

Come on, thought Lewis.You know exactly why we're stopping. But you're asking me why. So I've got to come up with some bullshit line on the evening sky.

'I thought we could stare at the stars for a while.'

'What stars? It's cloudy.'

'A mere technical hitch.' He smiled before continuing. 'Well perhaps we can wind down the windows and listen to the wind whining through the electricity pylons.'

Louise laughed lightly and then turned and kissed him.

'I know why we came up here. I just wanted to know what you would say.'

'I'm hurt that you could think such a thing.'

He smiled before asking. 'How did I do?'

'Not bad, pretty corny, but reasonably original.'

As they kissed again he thought that the evening might have been worth the effort after all.

'And where do you think you're going?'

Louise was becoming disturbingly straightforward. The coy smiles and subtle flirtations of consecutive Saturday nights had been sucked away with the rest of the simple facade.

'I'm trying to squeeze over into your seat but the gear stick is in the way.' Lewis joined her game. His was getting him nowhere.

'I thought you were supposed to be shy.'

'Who gave you that idea?'

'You did.'

'I must have been drunk.'

'You were,' Louise confirmed.

'Well I'm sober now and my intentions are purely sexual,' he confirmed, hoping to sound reasonably sincere.

'Well I'll permit you this once,' she said candidly.

This was an unusual game. Lewis was intrigued. People behave unexpectedly when their legs are open. He continued kissing Louise while he moved his hand across the front of her loose jumper. She kissed him harder. Encouraged, he caressed her breast with more confidence, feeling the softness through the wool. She still kissed him, so he moved his hand beneath her jumper, touching her warm skin.

'Your hands are cold,' she whispered. They continued kissing.

Lewis felt the tension drift over him as he touched the rounded softness of her breasts caught beneath the nylon. He forced himself harder against her but he could only feel the rough insensitivity of denim. The suggestion of the position gave the excitement.

He moved his right hand across the front of her jeans, stopping on the tight metal of the zip. His fingers fumbled with the button. Removing tight denims in the front seat of a volkswagen requires application. Lewis was prepared to apply himself. The zip was undone and Lewis was about to slip his fingers between her legs when she pulled his hand away. His hard-on collapsed under the pressure of his jeans as their brief intimacy dissipated into the mist that swirled around the car. The excitement had gone. He tried again to make sure, but it had gone. He didn't try hard to conceal his disappointment. He was relieved when Louise broke off the kissing.

'I think we'd better go now, it's getting late.'

'Are you sure?' he asked, trying to sound surprised and reluctant, but not so reluctant that he might receive a reprieve. He didn't want to endure twenty minutes of aimless kissing.

'Yes, I've got work in the morning.'

'Aye, and me. We'd better go then.'

'Yes.'

Lewis levered himself back into the driver's seat, adeptly avoiding the gear-stick and steering wheel. Louise discreetly refastened her jeans and straightened her jumper without speaking further to Lewis.

The car shivered in frigid cordiality. Lewis had experienced worse endings to an evening, but there had been sex involved.

The car reluctantly ground back into life. Lewis had taken care to park facing down a slope but unusually gravity wasn't required.

The lights of the town spun away in the distance of the valley and across the marsh to the river and further beyond that to the sea where Lewis, if he had looked, would have seen the lights of a dredger sucking sand from the wandering channels. The view was a cameo before the road plunged back down the mountain into the woods and onto the town beyond.

They did not speak as the car laboured its way across town towards Louise's house. Lewis was content to listen to the local radio station as it faded on and off the dial. He had meant to buy a new set but hadn't motivated himself as yet.

'Daniel Street, isn't it?'

'Yes.'

'How far along?'

'Just past that red car if you can.'

'Sure.'

Lewis stopped the car but kept the engine running. She was unlikely to ask him to sit on a settee with a sister or two. He was bored with settees anyway.

'Will I see you again?' she asked.

'Course you will.'

'When?'

'I'll be out Saturday night.'

She turned and kissed him before the open door illuminated their thoughts. The door slammed and he watched her turn and run across the road. She rang a doorbell attached to a door on a small terraced house. A light came on. Lewis drove away.

THURSDAY

'John Long's carpets, unbea...'
  'Two fifty seven swa...'

'Lewis, love.'

'The next record...'

'Lewis, it's seven.'
'Nothing ever happens, nothing...'
'We all go along as before.'
'And that was from...'
'Next the....after this.'
'Breakfast is....Baker hire this week.'
'At the Enterprise Zone, a free microwave oven.'

'Are you up yet?'
'Uh?'
'It's seven-thirty.'
'I'll be up now.'

Lewis focused hazily across the room, his gaze directed by
the dull light feebly dripping through the curtains. The green
unreal glow of the radio alarm clock flickered malevolently in
the darkest corner. It joyfully informed him that it was seven o
six. As usual it was wrong; who can you trust when your clock
lies to you? The radio offered him another microwave he didn't
need. He realised he would have to get up. Another reality
filled morning was there waiting. It was not about to go away

13

through lack of attention. Winter nights are the shortest when you are counting the hours. Sunday was still three days away. At least he didn't have a hangover.

He forced the overbearing weight of the quilt off the bed and stood up with as much reluctance as he could muster without actually staying in bed. His eyes refocused inaccurately as he reached for a pair of jeans hung over the back of the room's solitary chair. It was a basic room: four walls and a ceiling; one floor; one cupboard brown and boring; an arched mirror; a relict desk from a time when he was supposed to have been a studious schoolboy and a piano which he never played. Lewis stumbled out of it and into the bathroom where a handful of cold water brought him completely out of the night for the first time.

After gingerly washing himself, Lewis made the descent to the breakfast table where he knew from experience his mother and father would already be. His mother was a phenomenon; her efficiency was frightening. She would have been up at six, never needing the extra sleep and by the time Lewis surfaced already washed the clothes, hung them out to dry, ironed the clothes she had aired yesterday, set the breakfast table and finally cut the sandwiches for both Lewis and his father's lunch. Lewis could only just manage sitting at the breakfast table, eating and perhaps making the odd brief attempt at conversation.

Nobody spoke as Lewis grappled heroically with an unco-operative piece of toast in a vain attempt to cover it with jam. Giving up, he concentrated on eating it.

'Still up at Longford?' His father asked him. He already knew the answer but was bored with the silence.

'Yeh,' replied Lewis through a mouthful of toast.

'How many weeks have you got left up there?' He knew the rough answer to this one as well but conversation with Lewis in the morning required patience.

'Three, perhaps four.'

'Been there a while now.'

'Yes, I'm bored stiff with the place.'

'Well, I did warn you didn't I?'

'What do you mean?'

'I told you not to join the building trade.'

'Leave it out, Dad.'

'It's alright saying leave it out, but I've told you before, you should have stayed on at school.' He had told him before. It was his favourite lecturing topic.

'Oh yeah, with one 'O' level in art. What the hell was I going to do?'

'That was your own decision, you know you could have...'

'Leave it out Dad, it's too bloody early in the morning.'

'Language, please,' his mother interrupted. 'You're not on the building site yet.'

'He'd never have need gone on the building site if he'd listened to what I told him.'

'David, please, that's enough.'

'I don't know why I put up with this. One mention of a complaint against the building game and he's off on his favourite ramble. I mean everybody complains about work but I have to get a lecture on bloody higher education.'

'Lewis,' her tone warned him not to continue. 'Pass your mother the jam.'

Lewis obliged.

Ten minutes later Lewis was walking down Pant Glas towards the junction with the main road. His boss would pick him up at ten past eight.

He shared the bus stop with two middle-aged women and a tall schoolgirl from the Catholic college. One of the women looked him up and down. He smiled hopefully at the girl, she ignored him. He consoled himself with the solace that she was too young anyway.

The schoolgirl boarded her bus and the women theirs but

there was still no sign of Watkins. J.R.Watkins:Jeremiah Royston Watkins. Lewis had been working for him for almost five years. It was a small operation: the boss, Lewis, and a plasterer brought in when the work was available. Roy was getting on a bit now: nearly sixty but he was still fit and as least as sharp as his plaster board nails. He struggled with the heavier work, forcing Lewis to work harder as a result. But he was fair and although Lewis described him as a hard bastard he rather liked him. The extra work was nothing.

A wide overweight van appeared in the distance beyond the traffic lights. As it meandered closer the legend blazoned brazenly across the front demanded attention. J.R.Watkins Master Builder. It still made Lewis smile, despite its accuracy.

The van slouched into the bus stop. J.R. would occasionally boast that he had been in business thirty years. The van looked as if it had seen twenty of them but it was only an illusion; nothing lasted long with Roy. Lewis was doing well on four.

'Morning, Roy,' offered Lewis as he jumped into the warm cab.

'Morning, Lew.'

Nobody ever addressed him as J.R. to his face. It was doubtful if he would have understood the Dallas connection. But you didn't take the chance. Most people called him Mr.Watkins with a reverence reserved for a religious man. Few knew what the J stood for. Lewis knew because it was on his income tax forms. He was doing well with Roy.

The van ambled back out into the flow of traffic. A cacophony of horns objected to its arbitrary progress. Roy was not one for the formalities of the highway code.

'They can run into me if they want to, Lew, but who's going to come off worse?'

The morning ambled forward. Lewis had mixed a banker for Roy to get on with before turning his attention to the ton of breeze blocks which had to be moved for the garage.

'Ready for breakfast, Lew?'

'Aye right, Roy,' replied Lewis eagerly.

'Get the tea on then.'

'Right.'

Lewis turned the cement mixer off and an unsuitable silence surrounded the site.

Breakfast was the first stoppage of the day. It wasn't really breakfast as both Lewis and Roy would have eaten earlier but it was a necessary break. Lewis carried the tea to the first floor where Roy had been working. Roy was sitting on an up-turned milkcrate earnestly reading the back page of the *Daily Mirror*. He didn't look up as Lewis placed a mug of tea in front of him.

'I see the Swans won last night,' announced Roy.

'Aye, I heard it on the radio this morning.'

'I thought you'd have gone down.'

'No, I haven't bothered much this season, with the rugby and all I haven't had much time,' explained Lewis.

'It's the women that's stopping you watching the football. I'll bet that's where you were last night,'

'Well as a matter of fact...'

Roy laughed.

'Who was it this time?'

'Just some girl I've been bumping into on the weekends.'

'Anyone I know?'

'You wouldn't know her, would you?'

'I might, mun, what's her name?'

'Louise.'

'C'mon, Lew, play the game, Louise what?'

'Richardson.'

'Where does she live?'

'Daniel Street, you don't know her,' Lewis insisted emphatically.

'Up above the old cinema?'

'Aye,'

'Is her father's name Dennis?'

There was a pause.

'I don't know.'

'Used to work in the steelworks before they laid him off.'

Lewis surrendered to his interrogator.

'Could be.'

'Her mother works on the fruit stall in the market?'

'How the hell am I supposed to know? Took her out I did, not research her life history.'

'I know her, mun, well I used to know her mother anyway. Gwen Williams, a right raver in her day, not that I'd know anything of that mind.'

Lewis marvelled at Roy's encyclopedic knowledge of the town's inhabitants.

'You'd better watch her, Lew.'

'I was, last night.'

Roy laughed.

'No joy then, Lew?'

Lewis said nothing.

'Thought you were looking a bit down this morning.'

Lewis remained silent. Roy laughed again.

'C'mon then, Lew, these walls won't build themselves. Another banker.'

Lewis was almost eager to get started again. The cement mixer grudgingly spluttered into its uneven laborious rotation, churning sand and cement which Lewis shovelled effortlessly into its wide gaping mouth.The work to him now was easy, laborious but easy. The tired ache of his muscles, taut on the warmest of mornings, was now only a distant memory of his first months with Roy. He had always been strong in comparison with his peers at school; his winning of the discus throwing at the school sports day was an annual event. He even had a certificate buried somewhere with his mother's patiently ambitious mementos of his youth. Lewis Davies West Glamorgan County Champion-Intermediate Level. The lettering was in gold and there was an underlain picture of a runner in silhouette. There had been speculation of winning a red vest, but there was training involved and he wouldn't discipline himself. What was the point? He had won the school championships out of fun: it was easy. The county championships because they involved a day off school. He had been surprised when he had won, narrowly but with no extra effort. Dai Sparks, the sports teacher, had been excited by his win, cajoling and then threatening him to train for a national vest. Lewis had known the distances required were beyond him and even if he could have achieved them after three months training, so what? He could throw a discus an extra 1.8 metres. Useful. He had enjoyed throwing it because it was an easy skill; training would have stifled the pleasure.

When he had abandoned school early in April, his body had recoiled from the intense strain enforced upon him. The building game was hard. He was strong but it was a raw shallow strength of early youth. His muscles flared with the extra exertion. Every shovel of sand, barrowful of cement and armful of breeze blocks burned his body further. But his strength was not a brittle strength; it diminished and then regrouped, his body hardening as the callouses on his hands hardened to enclose his first watery blisters. Now, after four years with Roy, the aches of the morning and the warm stinging blisters of the afternoons were only a distant laughing memory.

He worked as a machine. It was rumoured among his friends that he ran on diesel. 'You only had to fill him up every half hour.' Lewis enjoyed the humour, people could look at his actions all they liked but no one could picture his thoughts.

He tipped the banker out of the mixer into the wheelbarrow, its regular consistency just supporting its own weight. It had a dull green colour: the beach yellow of the quartz sand overwhelmed by a grey glutinous cement. When Lewis was killing time he would occasionally pick a shell fragment from the sand and idly recall its provenance, memorised from his geology lessons. The subject had always fascinated him. The time scales were somehow reassuring: a sandstone 250 million years old; a mollusc 350 million years old. It demanded a perspective. He was only twenty years old; how was it possible to reconcile the scales except in terms of a hopelessly brief life. Everlasting life in death was not an alternative. He quoted faultlessly from an 'O' level text book concerning a 300 million year dead shell when in a mere sixty years there would be no mind. The mountains upon which he spent most of his youth were continually in the motion of rejoining the sea from which they had only recently come. It was all a cycle and for him it would be a brief one.

'Oi! Lew, What's the bloody hold-up? Are you catching a bus to mix that cement?'

Roy's voice disturbed Lewis from a discussion with himself. He realised with disgust that he was killing time. The work was strangling him. He quickly filled two buckets with cement before making the short journey to the upstairs extension where Roy was completing an inside screen wall.

'Come on, Lew, where the hell have you been?'

'Sorry, Roy, couldn't get the mix right.'

Roy knew this wasn't the real reason. He looked at the boy with guilt but just took the buckets of cement. Not wishing to interfere, Roy sensed the disillusionment that Lewis was experiencing. He had lived it. It had taken him twenty years to work through. He just hoped it would not take Lewis that long. A few more years on the piss with the lads, a couple of seasons of rugby, a rushed romance of living room floors and car front seats hiding from parents and the blaze of headlights. And then a woman to look after him before the easy nights absorbed him. Roy watched Lewis out of the window space as he walked back to the mixer. He hoped Lewis could hack it: he liked him. He stayed when most drifted on. He worked hard and he could talk, not just about the building game and rugby, he had ideas.

Roy had watched Lewis grow up. He remembered the boyish enthusiasm of the first weeks at work, willing to learn despite the tired muscles. He had been impressed by his subtle adaptions to the toil of work. Then he watched, fascinated as

Lewis let his thoughts appear; always much closer to the surface than he realised and a mirror image of his own thirty years ago. The disillusionment with the cycle of work, the endless repetition and the awful realisation that there was nothing else. Life was this. Roy stood back as Lewis would attempt to bury his thoughts, subjugate with distractions his frustrated ideas. Futile pursuits would distort his time: sport, women, beer. Usually it would be drink. Equilibrium would be grudgingly regained as his goals tasted of distaste. Commitment altered little and hid nothing.

To Roy it was absorbing. A chance to reassess his own youth, gauge his own mistakes from a cheap ringside seat. He did not interfere, allowing Lewis to make his own decisions, mark his own time. Roy knew himself too well; he wouldn't have listened.

His own first days at work were not that far away. The unfamiliar faces with the more than familiar practical jokes; he had learned to laugh early but embarrassment is difficult to conceal, anger even harder. He had finished school on a Friday and started work the following Monday. His mother had arranged the apprenticeship for him. There had been no question of staying on, with younger brothers to support. His father was a hazy memory, a smiling face in black and white, holding his mother in a bare studio. The coal had taken him away before Roy had a chance to learn to know him. There was only a lingering happiness, of huge warm hands as they threw him into the air before engulfing him in a sea of strength. The board had settled with free coal for a lifetime in an attempt to ameliorate for the loss. The compensation was less because his soul had clung to a burnt body and a determined wife for a few days outside the mine.

The apprenticeship was with Will Davies. His mother had insisted on a Saturday start: there was no point in hiding from work. Will had sent him away. 'Don't start anyone on a Saturday, son. Come back Monday, eight sharp. Have the weekend off on me.' Roy never started anything on a Saturday.

Roy didn't blame his mother for forcing him to work. She had no alternative. But it still hurt when he was tricked into thinking about it. He wouldn't have been good enough for a scholarship, but he was brighter than the majority of boys whose fathers had been able to pay for grammar school. Education was only free if you could afford it. Free for the boys who now worked in town, cocooned in corpulent offices, or had moved away to another provincial retreat as lethargic as the last. There was resentment in that there had been no opportunity for him. He had to make his own way or be entrapped in the benefit maze or submerged in the cheap rotten beer that would hold so many of his once friends. Shadow figures in a grey half awake town.

Roy knew that Lewis hadn't seen the chances in school, a way forward. Lewis had hated the regimented dullness, the concerted attempt to homogenize everyone in the mire of reduced expectation. There was an opportunity there; an escape route if you wanted it enough. Roy would have exploited it but there were no first chances. While the dullards with the money had prospered and now offered platitudes to him across stained desks, as he paid for the handshakes and signatures. Smiles through transparent bars.

Roy was aware that Lewis's father had made a vain attempt to force Lewis to stay on at school, vaguely aware of the advantages. Roy would have done better but rarely questioned Lewis on his decision. Mark his own time, make his own mistakes.

Roy levelled the next course of breeze-blocks against his line. Lewis had kept him regularly supplied with cement and blocks. When he was working he didn't like to move far for anything. It disturbed his thoughts, the subtle conversation with himself. The background grind of the cement mixer faded, reminding Roy that it would soon be lunch-time. He had to finish the wall by lunch.

'Do you want some chips, Roy?'

'No thanks, Lew, Iris has made me some sandwiches.'

'Well it's ten to, so I'm off down the chippy. Sure you don't want anything?'

'No, I'm fine.'

Roy listened to the back gate being unlatched before returning to finish the wall before lunch-time, finish another wall before another lunch-time.

Roy settled himself onto one of the inverted milkcrates that doubled as a seat and a stand for makeshift scaffolding. Lunch-time gave him a chance to rest. A time to assess the morning's work and gauge how far he had got, which was invariably not as far as he wanted to be. It was a pleasure for Lewis to listen to Roy pick over a successful week on a Friday afternoon. But it was another day before Friday and an urgency had entered their work in an attempt to finish things before the weekend. They didn't like to carry a week's work forward; it disrupted the rhythm.

Lewis used his donkey jacket to soften the wooden floor but he still shuffled uncomfortably as he ate from his tray of beans and chips. Roy picked at his sandwiches, half listening to the radio's partial news coverage, the reader's voice switching effortlessly from the war in Iran to a local councillor's pronouncements on the provision of better bus services to council estates. The alacrity of topic changes was somehow reassuring. Roy was aware of the insignificance of it all; nothing mattered at all.

'Do you want some tea, Lew?'

'No thanks, Roy, I got a coke from the shop.'

Roy poured himself a cup of tea out of a battered teapot which had faithfully followed him around various building sites. He preferred a site where there was some electricity to boil a kettle. He didn't like tea out of a flask: it never tasted the same. When he had to he carried a small bottle of milk with his lunch box to pour into his tea. Milk in a flask always strangled the tea. Except on the colder days Lewis had not yet developed Roy's enthusiasm for tea and by lunch-time he craved cold fluids to replace the sweat he would have lost during the morning. Tea was a passion with Roy; he would remember good sites by the quality of the tea made by the owner or a friendly neighbour. He would cultivate potential tea providers at a new site with a rare charm and flow of compliments which would guarantee regular breakfast and lunch cuppas and occasionally a mid-afternoon one. Roy could recognise different teas and even the various brands by taste.Tea-bags were frowned upon unless there was no alternative, when he would cheerfully complain about the taste of the bag but drink it all the same. His incipient Buddhism lapsed in a preference for china cups, especially when served on a tray.

The tea situation on this site was lousy. The couple he was doing the job for both worked. There were no friendly neighbours and tea bags were a necessity.

'This tea is too bloody weak to get out of the pot. Who bought this stuff?'

'You did, Roy.'

'Couldn't have, Iris must have; I'd have never bought this. The tea is terrible on this site. I'll be glad when we're off this one, Lew.'

'Perhaps we'll have better luck on the next site, Roy.'

'Aye, another site like that one in Gorseinon would be just right. Remember that one, Lew?'

'The one with the tea urn?'

'Yes, that was a site. He used to fill it up in the morning and there would be hot tea all day. Great site that, I enjoyed it there.'

Lewis remembered the site clearly. There had been gallons of the stuff to tide them over a couple of cold months. He had been forced to take a piss six times a day on account of the amount of tea he was drinking. He also suspected that they had prolonged the job a month longer than was necessary on account of the prodigious amount of tea available. Roy was never in a rush to get off a good tea site. Finishing a job quickly for the money was never important to him. He had the sites well worked out; he knew how long he could take and he took his own time. Lewis enjoyed this attitude to work; he admired Roy for it. They only rushed when it was necessary for the people they were building for.

'What about that site up on Church Road?'

'Aye, remember that? We couldn't get away from there quick enough. It was undrinkable.'

'You had to drink it though.'

Roy smiled at Lewis as he recalled the taste. It was etched onto his palate. Lewis had poured potfuls of the brown liquid masquerading as tea into an ungrateful privet hedge, while Roy had tried desperately to conceal the fact that he was fetching a flask into work. His charm had worked to perfection. The elderly widow for whom they were building an extension had taken to Roy instantly and religiously supplied him with copious amounts of perfectly undrinkable tea. Roy, unable to hurt her feelings, had been forced into swallowing it in large gulps while the happy widow chatted amiably to him on the backdoorstep. Poor tea to a Buddhist is purgatory and without crossing faiths the bags were being re-used.

'Want some crisps, Roy?'

'No thanks, Lew. Iris is trying to put me on a diet. Crisps are off, I think.'

Lewis extended the almost empty packet before up-ending it and letting the remainder slide into his mouth.

'Training tonight, Lew?'

'No, I'm going to give it a miss tonight, stay in instead. I'm a bit knackered.'

'You've a big game on Saturday, haven't you?' Surprise evident in Roy's question.

'Aye, Dunvant.'

'Top of the league, aren't they?'

'Aye.'

'And you need the points or you're going to be relegated.'

'We could do with the win.'

'Well why aren't you training then? It's hardly the attitude for a big game, is it?' admonished Roy.

'Aw, I'm pissed off with the whole set-up. No bugger trains, why should I? Take it, there'll be about eight firsts out tonight and some hopefuls from the seconds. Where the hell is that going to get us?'

'Yes, but if you don't train there'll be seven firsts.'

'I know that, Roy, but the attitude isn't there. It's the same ones training and the same ones skiving. But they'll still pick the bastards come selection tonight.'

'Why don't you say something then?'

'I do Roy but it doesn't get you anywhere, and it'll be the bloody committee who'll moan come Saturday when Dunvant put thirty on us. And then they'll go and drop the ones who have been training.'

'You should stand for captain next season then,' suggested Roy hopefully. He considered that Lewis would make a good captain, given the opportunity, and perhaps it would provide a focus to direct his energy. He guessed that the building trade was only tiring him, nothing constructive.

'No thanks, I couldn't stand the hassle. Committee meetings, selection grievances, match postmortems. I can do without all that. Anyway, they can stuff their training. Tonight I'm staying in.'

'Staying in with anyone particular, Lew? Louise Richardson perhaps?' Roy hadn't forgotten his earlier conversation and was eager to find out more on Louise Richardson.

'No, I don't think so, Roy. I won't be seeing her again, or not until I'm six pints under anyway.' Lewis was more relaxed now that he had aired his grievance over the running of the club.

'Why's that then?' asked Roy, anticipating the answer.

'She was a bit forward.'

Roy's laughter forced a smile from Lewis before he elaborated.

'She was alright, even a bit of a laugh, but there was this vague feeling that we weren't really suited and would never really be at ease with each other.'

'That's rather a sweeping statement for the first date, Lew. Give the girl a chance; perhaps she was shy.'

'She wasn't shy. In fact she was straightforward, disturbingly straightforward. Up to a point.'

'What happened after the point?'

'She closed up.'

'What were you expecting, a quick leg over in the back of your wagon?'

'No. The front would have done. I mean my best lines all evening and she still wouldn't take me serious until it got serious.'

'It sounds to me, Lew, she was just a bit too sharp for you.'

'Well she won't be seeing the inside of my car for a while,' predicted Lewis.

'I'll bet she'll be heartbroken,' replied Roy unconvincingly.

Lewis smiled as he got up. He enjoyed Roy's playful teasing.

The images of the evening intrigued him. Louise was not the girl he remembered from beery Saturday nights in the Cherub. But his general recollections of any Saturday night were usually blurred, filled with things which may have happened but probably hadn't and others which he wished he could forget. But his exuberant charm must have worked because she had agreed to go out with him mid-week. He normally avoided mid-week dates as it suggested the build up to a relationship. Sex would have had something to do with it; in fact it would have provided the prime motivation. His sex life was at best an occasional occurrence and had recently confined itself to making guest appearances, usually on some worn living-room carpet or badly sprung settee. The summer was more accommodating but open fields on the mountainside never appeared to hold the same romantic appeal to his girlfriends as him. Summer fields evoked memories of Marianne, but Lewis had carefully reburied these. Exhumation came only in flashes as the soil gently shifted. He quickly forgot again.

Lewis continued to mix cement while the afternoon meandered lazily along like a tired river. He allowed the sounds of the building site to engulf him: the mixer's truculent churning; the clean sharp slice of the shovel through sand and the harsher wet sound through saturated cement. A radio played apathetically on the first floor, unwilling to compete with the mixer, while occasionally a raised voice suspended in mid-conversation drifted in from another house in the small cul-de-sac where they were working.

They didn't stop working during the afternoon. It would always be a straight run through to consolidate the morning's work or catch up if they were behind. According to Roy they were always behind. It did that to you, working for yourself, but he never worried about it. Lewis would follow the progress of the afternoon through the half-hourly news bulletins on the radio and then by the stream of children walking home from the local primary school. Wherever they worked, a scattering of children would magically appear at around twenty to four as they chased their way home, released from the constraints of another day at school. Lewis sometimes envied them, especially the younger ones, laughing their way through an uncomplicated existence. School and home life all planned. Naive in their assurance, not doubting the simplicity of living. Lewis didn't remember his own childhood very well. But then who does?

The news on the radio at four would signal a winding down for the day. He would rarely mix another after four. The site would have to be cleaned up. Roy hated leaving an untidy site especially if someone was living in a house onto which they were building an extension. He didn't like working in a mess and he didn't want anyone to live in one. Lewis would then prepare the site for the following morning. Friday had gained in significance throughout the day. Lewis had realised Roy's work plan: if they didn't get on they would be back in on Saturday morning. Neither of them enjoyed Saturday morning working but Roy was in an uncharacteristic rush to finish the site. The tea was lousy.

'Ready then, Lew?'

'Aye, everything set.'

'Cleared up?'

'Aye.'

'Washed the mixer?'

'Aye.'

'Put the tools in the van?'

'All there.'

'Right then, let's get home, is it?'

It was the same conversation every night. Lewis had always cleared away and Roy knew it, but they still followed the same ritual.

They climbed into the van leaving the strangely inactive building site to await their return and departure on another day.

Roy dropped off Lewis where he had picked him up in the morning. The same workers who had been rushing in eight hours earlier were now scurrying home again. Home to a safe haven, to food, to a lover, to an enemy; perhaps to no one. What is there to do on a weekday evening? Bachelors phoning their friends for a drink while the married ones turn on a chat show. The walk home is always shorter with the experience of another working day past but the relief is always tainted with the knowledge of another one waiting in the morning. How long does it take?

Lewis was hungry. The need to eat focused his attention; if he didn't eat soon he would have to wait until after training.

A light in the kitchen held out against the enveloping darkness. His father was already home and reading the evening paper. He barely looked up as Lewis opened the door. They then embarked on a routine question exchange in which neither listened to the replies. Lewis's mother had not yet returned from her job as a typist in the civic centre. Lewis selected a complete meal from the freezer. The instructions on the packet advised him to cook for five minutes on defrost and then for five on full power. Lewis set the microwave for ten minutes on full power; it would even out.

Lewis didn't like the microwave but he used it. It was easy: there was no need to think. His father had returned to the paper. The purr of the microwave was punctuated by the turn of printed pages. Lewis stood and waited.

'Make us a cup of tea, Lew.'

Lewis made two mugs of tea and sat down opposite his father with his microwaved dinner.

'Going training tonight, Lew?'

'Aye, might as well, Dad. There's nothing else to do.' He had used up his anger with Roy lunchtime. He was not going to go over it again.

'Dunvant Saturday, isn't it?'

'Aye.'

His father abandoned further attempts at conversation returning to the paper as a better alternative. There used to be a warmth between them that had slowly cooled over the years, stifled by the absence of new shared experiences. You can't maintain a friendship on memories alone. They were no more than cordial housemates who had the obligatory but not defining relationship of father and son. The disagreement over breakfast was already forgotten, but it all contributed to an accumulating feeling of distance between them. His father traced this to the fierce arguments over Lewis leaving school. He had fostered hopes of Lewis succeeding in school. There had even been a few reasonable end of year reports. The idea of Lewis leaving early had angered him as he was unable to comprehend why. His plans foundered during Lewis's final year with a threat of expulsion over a dispute with a chemistry teacher; an affair that remained unexplained despite a visit to the headmaster's office. Lewis was eventually suspended for a fortnight. The suspension killed any enthusiasm that Lewis had possessed for the school. He attended only sporadically up until Easter when at the first opportunity he left officially, returning only to complete and sit his art exam. There was to be no sixth form. When the results were announced in August, Lewis had passed his art with an A grade. It was on this result that his father based a whole theory of squandered academic excellence. He extolled this theory for almost a year until the arguments were threatening violence. His wife, in tears, pleading with him, had convinced him to stop but the disappointment still swilled around unable to find a drain into the past where it could become absorbed and forgotten. Lewis hated to be reminded as he had far from forgotten. A resentment still lingered but it was not something he could explain to his father.

'Your mother will be home soon, Lew.'

'Yes, she should be here now.'

'Put the kettle on for her then.'

'It's just boiled.'

'Go on. She'll be here any minute.'

'She's not here yet.'

Before Lewis could again postpone the inevitable cup of tea the sound of a key searching for an entrance into the front door announced the arrival of his mother. He reluctantly rose from the table. The paper hid his father's smile.

'Hello, I'm home.'

'Hi'ah, Mam.'

'Give us a hand with the shopping, love.'

His mother struggled in through the front door with two hopelessly overfilled carrier bags.

'Didn't know you were going to Tescos tonight, Mam,' queried Lewis as he relieved his mother of her shopping bags.

'I wasn't going to but Majorie offered me a lift. Anyway, it'll save the rush tomorrow night.'

'I don't know why you bother on a Friday night. It's as if the whole bloody town is there.'

'They usually are, love, but if I don't get it who will?'

There was no objection to this question. Lewis's father surfaced briefly from the paper before resubmerging himself in it. The chances of either of them helping with the weekly shopping were remote; his father had ventured as far as the multi-storey car park while Lewis had actually braved the building on a few notable occasions. He had not enjoyed the experience. The place had been packed: the people as close together as the tins, packets and boxes bordering the narrow corridors that bludgeoned you into buying. He had twisted memories of attempting to manoeuvre an unwieldy trolley through a swarm of other trolleys all of which were apparently travelling in the opposite direction to him and handled by evidently more experienced operators. He had become involved in two minor altercations and there had been an abundance of aggrieved looks as he battered his way around the carefully designed supermarket. He had been on the verge of abandoning the trolley and heading for the nearest pub, conveniently across the road, but his mother had coerced him into staying with threats of not washing his kit. When he had finally negotiated the obstacle course he was faced with a depressingly long queue which diminished at a soporific rate. He had left the supermarket thoroughly tense and agitated, swearing never to enter the place on a Friday night again. His mother had aborted her plans of allowing him to go alone. He was amazed how people returned after the first attempt. Perhaps like sex they were hoping it was going to get better after a disappointing opening. After a week of accumulating frustration at work and simmering tensions at home, they subjected themselves to shopping at Tescos. You could probably trace the majority of domestic violence to shopping at Tescos followed by eight pints down the pub. Lewis thought that he would probably have to kill someone if he was forced to endure it every week. Fortunately he didn't have to as his mother did it for him. He gave her thirty pounds every Friday night and everything else fell into place. There was always food in the fridge, his clothes were washed, aired and ironed, the heating was on when he came home, all the bills were paid. And they never ran out of toilet paper. Lewis rarely considered the practicalities of the situation or the amount of work involved: an attitude inherited from his father, who allowed the running of the house to pass over him with the calm assurance that it was no concern of his. The effort was daunting. But no one noticed except on the rare occurrences when she was ill: it simply collapsed. Lewis had no wish to understand how efficiently she worked. He was happy to pay the thirty pounds on a Friday night, aware that he was getting a good deal but not wishing to know how good lest it disappear.

'Put the bags here for you, Mam?'

'Yes please love.'

'Shall I put them away for you, Mam?'

His mother smiled.

'No thank you, love, I'll do it now.'

Lewis deposited the carrier bags on the kitchen unit. He briefly thought about asking her if she needed anything else done but dismissed it on the possibility that she did.

'Well I'm off training in a minute. I've just got to put my kit together.'

There was no reply which Lewis took as an indication that he was not needed. He abandoned the kitchen to the efficient silence of his mother which was broken only by the rustle of newsprint as his father flicked through the paper.

A dim security light faltered in the weak drizzle which darkened the tarmac of the club car park. Lewis waited patiently, reluctant to leave the warmth of his car. He counted three other vehicles. He knew the drivers and acknowledged Mike in the car next to him. He speculated, eight players here now, perhaps another six who would turn up. Fuck, what was he doing here? Another set of headlights illuminated the drizzle before a fat Ford Granada lumbered up outside the club building. The driver's door opened and the occupant disembarked with an air of importance that should have precluded his entry to anywhere as unglamorous as a rugby club on a Thursday night.

'Well at least that bastard's here,' commented Lewis to

himself in the absence of anyone else in the car.

'Had to really, I suppose. He's got the bloody keys.'

Although it had been known to wait an hour for somebody to open the changing rooms.

The figure from the Granada walked disdainfully to the side entrance of the club building which abutted onto an open field, its boundaries lost from view in the drizzled darkness. The changing room light elicited a similar response from the cars, flashing on then off again as the occupants made a dash for the club. Lewis was last to enter. The white-washed walls forced his eyes to readjust to the brightness just too quickly as a series of greetings and abuse greeted him.

'Awright, Lew?'

'Hi'ah Mike.'

'Hi'ah, Lew.'

'Lew.'

'Awright, pal.'

'What a night for training, ay.'

Lewis tried to instill some enthusiasm into his voice that he didn't feel. There was no reply – it was a mutual feeling. He settled down into the corner of the changing room, unwilling to begin undressing and start the training ordeal. He stared in isolation at a piece of dried mud on the bare concrete floor. The changing room hadn't been cleaned since Saturday and the desiccated mud, discarded from a boot in the aftermath of a match now lay brittle on the floor. A number of petrified circular shapes betrayed its provenance. Lewis's eyes remained fixed upon it, already a relic from a long-forgotten never-recalled match. He wondered how much mud had been swept away from the changing room every week for thirty years. Thirty years of endeavour in the search of enjoyment. How many more countless Saturday afternoons? He spat viciously at the dried mud, his saliva forming globules which rolled and stuck in the dust. He rubbed the saliva and dried earth into the concrete floor with his trainer and watched as the brittle mud became malleable again.

'Ay Lew, you getting changed or what?'

The sharp question roused him from his reverie. He looked up resignedly.

'Aye, I suppose I better had,' he replied without any conviction. He was still reluctant to leave the warmth of his clothes and the soft heat of his thoughts.

Most of the other lads were changing, but there was no urgency in their actions. No one really wanted to train, not tonight. It was cold, wet and miserable; the enthusiasm was infectious. They were all ill with it. Reluctance pervaded every movement and spoken word. The season had become a burden, it had not been a good one. Relegation beckoned unless they won on Saturday but no one cared anymore. The majority didn't even train now. The boys who persevered loved the game or at least loved their wives less. Training was a good excuse for an evening's escape. For the unmarried ones it was a useful time filler before they ventured into town, always good for a laugh on a Thursday night.

The scrape of aluminium on the cold, earth-covered floor mingled with the occasional comment and meaningless banter that vied uneasily with the silence, as the varied occupants of the changing room changed into their one unifying element: rugby players.

'Anyone coming out?' Mike enquired to no one in particular. There was no reply.

'C'mon, boys, let's get out there.'

Lewis would have gone but he hadn't finished lacing his boots.

'Give it five, mun, Mike. It's bloody freezing out there,' requested a squat man through the tangle of an improbable beard.

Lewis looked up at Rod and smiled in admiration. Rod was a regular; he turned up every week. In fact he had turned up every week for the last fifteen years. He was well into his thirties and still enjoyed the game. But it was an admiration tinged with horror at the inevitability of it all. Would he really be doing this for that long, there had to be some progression. Well, there was always the committee.

Lewis tied up his thoughts with his bootlaces.

'C'mon, then, let's get it over with.'

There was a shuffle towards the door. Mike had already gone out and was now kicking the ball high up into the air and catching it again. The remainder of the occupants of the changing room gave in to the inevitable and trudged out onto the field.

Lewis felt the drizzle absorb him in its soft wetness as it clung to his jersey and the hairs on his legs. The weak training lights struggled to illuminate the pitch, one corner was almost dark where one of the bulbs had failed while the remainder of the pitch was bathed in a half light that endeavoured to keep the darkness at its edges. Around the lights the drizzle appeared to form concentric circles as the specks drifted to the ground. Towards the end of the season the pitch, never lavishly turfed, suffered through over-use and degenerated into a treacherous quagmire. The remaining isolated patches of grass caught the drizzle which then shimmered in the reflected lustre of the floodlights.

A number of players teed balls up on the mud before attempting to kick them between the uprights. The efforts were of widely varying quality, the big forwards illustrated clearly why they were never given the honour on a Saturday afternoon with a variety of grasscutters, improbable hooks and wide slices. While Saturday's regular kicker proceeded to demonstrate that without the pressure of a game and a crowd he could sail the conversions effortlessly through the uprights. But come Saturday when the real thing presented itself he would once again be reduced to an erratic hit and hope merchant.

Lewis wasn't interested in the kicking. He was realistic about his chances of having a go on Saturday and as a result he stood around, waiting for something more interesting to happen. He exchanged a few platitudes with some of the players who were waiting for a spare ball to kick at the posts but no one was interested in conversation.

'Game of touch, boys?' proposed Mike hopefully. There was little response. One or two heads turned but most of the fourteen or so players continued with aimless conversion practice.

Mike tried again. 'Let's get a game going, boys.' His suggestion again met with a muted response. But a few bodies gradually began to drift towards the centre of the pitch. Mike sensed his chance; announced with some authority. 'Stripes against plains, then.'

Everyone instinctively looked at their jerseys to see what side they were on. 'Stripes up that end.'

Two sides gradually separated to their respective halves of the pitch except Daz, the regular kicker, who was still trying to redeem himself for Saturday's dreadful miss in front of the post by kicking conversions from increasingly unlikely angles. Nobody was watching him, however, as Alfie Edwards was hovering nervously around the halfway line undecided over which side to join.

'What's up, Alfie?' questioned Mike, who was busily giving his side the game plan.

'Well, I'm not sure what side I'm on.'

There was a general round of laughter at Alfie's pronouncement. Alfie wasn't sharp and it showed.

'Well what jersey have you got on?' asked Mike in disbelief.

'Well it's sort of banded,' replied Alfie defensively to more general laughter.

'Up here, mun, Alfie,' shouted one of the stripes. Alfie, relieved to receive an instruction, began to jog up towards the stripes when one of the plains shouted.

'Don't listen to them, Alf, you're on our side, down 'ere, mun.'

Alfie stopped, engulfed in agonies of indecision.

'No, up 'ere mun Alf, stripes you've got on.'

'Down 'ere Alf.'

'C'mon Alfie, you're on our side.'

'Don't desert us, Alf.'

There was a general humour in the banter that Alfie missed completely. Lewis smiled in sympathy with Alfie but was unable to prevent himself from enjoying his predicament.

Mike settled the issue. 'You're on our side, Alfie: we're one short.'

The comments died away as Alfie joined the plains. Mike shouted for the ball which Daz reluctantly kicked to him. The game was about to start when someone objected to the arbitrary make-up of the sides. Lewis would have given up at this point but Mike persevered through another two minutes of argument during which Dai Philips changed sides twice before the game finally started.

Touch rugby was a favourite on a Thursday night. It involved little effort and almost no physical contact. It was hardly useful training for the match on Saturday but then nobody pretended it was.

The game had only been going five minutes when Lewis noticed a rotund figure in an ill-fitting tracksuit emerge from the changing rooms. It was Dai Fats; the name encapsulated his appearance. It wasn't that he was overweight; he was weight. His tracksuit failed miserably to cover his belly which protruded in the form of a large spherical object and had all the characteristics of a stick-on appendage. Fats was someone who put a lot of time and effort into his physique. He could usually be found propping up the bar on a time-share basis, but was known to avoid the training pitch with a rare commitment despite his nominal role as club coach. Fats was a dying breed: a dinosaur of a coach soon to be replaced by fitness coordinators and physios who ran leisure centres in their spare time. Most of the other teams already had a reputable coach: someone with first-class experience or even a minor ex-international. Fats's qualifications were based on a few unsuccessful youth team appearances before he graduated to the beery slob and barstool expert which he was now. In addition to a total lack of appreciation for the game he viewed most matches through an alcohol haze which was duly reflected in his training techniques and subsequent team selections. But although Fats stuck to his title with a rare resolution, in reality he knew he was on the way out and this season's imminent relegation would seal it. He had probably already settled for a selectorial role on the committee.

As he waddled closer several of the players realised with horror who he was and the game of touch gradually slowed to a standstill. He hadn't been out for a few weeks, citing a strained back muscle and he had never been known to come out on a Thursday. But he was no mirage. Down to his black and white bobble cap protecting his diminishing head of hair he was real and striding purposefully towards them, obviously intent on a last ditch attempt to avert relegation and maintain his personal source of international tickets.

Dai Fats needlessly announced his arrival on the field with a sharp blast on a whistle. The players shuffled around uneasily.

'Right then, four laps to warm up,' he bellowed across the pitch.

Mike jogged off instantly and the others grudgingly followed him while complaining bitterly to each other over the presence of Fats. There were not enough players to go through any meaningful practice moves while a fitness session with the game two days away would be useless. Lewis kept his thoughts to himself. He was aware of the futility of Fats's appearance but was still encouraged by his presence.

They knocked off the four laps easily with only two stragglers falling behind a comfortable pace. Fats stood motionless on the halfway line, only his head following the players progress as they ran around the perimeter of the pitch. As they jogged in, Fats imperiously announced a series of indeterminate sprints. Lewis could feel the reluctance stifle his stride as he accelerated the thirty yards of sprinting distance. An aversion to the training hung malignantly between the players. They were the ones out on a Thursday night and here they were getting bollocked for it.

Fats stood impassively on the halfway line periodically blasting his whistle between hoarse shouts of disparagement at the players' efforts.

'You're all too bloody slow,' he announced. 'No wonder you're bottom of the league.'

'I'd like to see that bastard come 'ere and try a sprint, just one,' cursed Daz.

'He's too fat to fucking run,' asserted Rod.

'Only time he runs is when it's his fucking round; you won't catch the bastard then.'

There was a round of laughter at the much abused joke.

'Right then, sixty yards now,' announced Fats with rancour coursing through his voice as he moved a further thirty yards away. The sprinting continued. Lewis was careful. He was fit: fit enough to cope with anything Fats could dream up and so were most of the boys. There was no point in killing themselves before the game on Saturday.

'Take it easy, boys; just stride it out. Don't worry about Fats; he'll soon head for the bar.'

Forty minutes later they were still running. The comments of muted disapproval had become threats of open mutiny. If they were to be believed a horrible death awaited Fats when he finally finished the training session. Fats had now resumed his position on the halfway line, his inert form occasionally bursting into a sequence of frenzied arm waving and side stretching. This he considered more than sufficient to maintain his fitness level. On this point, for one of the rare occasions in his life, he was right.

'Come on in then, boys. I want to say a few words about Saturday's game.'

The players reluctantly converged on Fats. A crowd shuffled around him, breathing heavily from their exertions. Viewed from a distance, the group appeared to be engulfed in a cloud of steam as their warm breath condensed in the sharp night air. Fats waited for a lull in the mutterings of discontent which lurked just below the surface of resentful attention. But as no lull appeared, he started his speech regardless.

'Right then, boys. You don't need me to tell you how fucking important this fucking game is for us on fucking Saturday.' Fats expected no reply and there wasn't any, save for a few embarrassed sideways glances. His use of adjectives was not extensive but he stuck with the ones he knew best and trusted. Fats continued. 'I've just got one fucking thing to say: if that fucking Dunvant outfit come up here Saturday thinking they can fucking win they've got another fucking think coming. Right?'

There was no reply to Fats in full flow. 'We're going to show them what fucking rugby in this valley is all about. We'll show them who can fucking play rugby. So get tuned in now and no fucking drinking on Friday night.'

With this final outline of Saturday's match plan Fats turned and headed for the bar. During the speech Lewis had difficulty containing his laughter which he had only drowned with a rising reservoir of contempt for the fallacy of the man.

'Right then, lads. We all know what we've got to do on Saturday: fuck them and there's no problem,' summarised Daz.

The group barely laughed as they gratefully made for the haven of the changing rooms. Only Mike remained to practice his kicking for Saturday.

The showers were a misnomer, involving only a tepid trickle of reluctant water. They were fitted in a hurry thirty years ago and might have been reasonable for a year or two but now only coughed and spluttered through rusting heads. It was necessary to get in early to catch the limited amount of water heated by the languid boiler, but even this was welcome after the long training session. Lewis relaxed under the weak but regular head he had claimed. The water splashed off his head and onto his back. The sensation was the most welcome of the evening. In the half-light he tried to remove as much mud as he could see.

'Coming down town tonight, Lew?' enquired Daz.

Lewis rinsed the shampoo from his eyes before replying.

'Where you thinking of going?'

'The Arch probably.'

'Aye, might as well, I suppose. Mike coming down?'

'No, I don't think so. He's saving his money for Saturday.'

'What for? It's his stag night, we'll be buying the drinks.'

'C'mon, Lew, you know his girlfriend. She won't let him out on a Thursday night with all those loose women around.'

'How does she know they're all loose?'

'That's where she met him, didn't she?' concluded Daz.

Lewis didn't reply, only smiled. 'I suppose he'll give us a lift into town though.'

'Aye, he should do. Ask him when he comes in.'

Lewis was half-dressed before Mike appeared in the changing rooms from his kicking practice. The showers were now cold.

'Ay, Mike, give us a lift into town will you?'

'Yeh sure, Lew. Going to leave your car here, are you?'

'Aye, I'll pick it up in the morning. We'll be in the bar, right.'

Lewis and Daz were just finishing their second pint when Mike joined them in the bar. Several of the boys had stayed for a swift drink but everyone except Daz and Lewis had departed after the first one. Dai Fats sat astride a stool while leaning against the bar for support. Selection would begin once the captain arrived. The barman gazed at the tv screen while Emlyn lost another show.

'You ready, boys?'

'Sure, unless you want one, Mike?'

'No, I'm alright. I've got to get home tonight. With the wedding a week away there's still a lot to sort out.'

'Fine, let's go then.'

Lewis climbed into the back seat of Mike's Ford Fiesta, pushing his briefcase and bag to one side. Mike was an audit clerk for the council. The briefcase was a present from his mother on passing his first set of professional examinations.

He found qualifications difficult but worked hard; his fiancée provided any shortfall in motivation. He could see the benefits of passing: a secure job with reasonable income and annual increments. It would pay the mortgage; he didn't want to think any further.

'You in, Daz?' affirmed Mike.

'I'm in. Let's go,' replied Daz.

Mike accelerated out of the car park, abandoning the club to its lonely vigil until Saturday afternoon when it would find its focus. Daz began an obligatory conversation.

'Nice car you've got here, Mike.'

'Do you want to buy it?'

'Why? You selling it?'

'Yes, I'm afraid so. I can't afford the loan repayments with a mortgage as well so I've got to get something cheaper. Fancy it?'

'No thanks, Mike. I don't think I could afford it either.'

'What about you, Lew?' enquired Mike.

Lewis who had only been partially listening to the conversation, scrambled for something to say. 'No thanks, Mike. My car's alright,' he replied, pardoning himself for not making an offer.

'You should get yourself a proper car, mun.'

'I couldn't afford a car like this. It's only you office types who buy these things.'

'Yeh, sure Lew,' replied Mike sarcastically. He was aware that Lewis would be earning at least as much as him at present: there would be cash in hand work and he was living with his mother. Lewis was far from short of a few quid but then that was his business and Mike allowed his sales pitch to lapse. He was resigned to advertising it in the paper. If only the wedding wasn't costing so much, or even a cheaper honeymoon.

The conversation trickled away as the radio asserted itself within the car. Bachelors ring up their friends for a drink.

Lyrics drifted in and out of his understanding as the car hugged the sides of the valley on its descent into town. Headlights periodically bared the interior as they outfaced cars struggling up the incline. From above, the town glowed in a blur of orange and white light. It could have been considered attractive. Its sullen countenance only became obvious as the road passed the sharp boundary between the outposted council estate and the sodden farmland not yet committed to new housing. The road pierced quickly into the centre of the town following the route of the old A48. Windsor Road, the old high street, still clung desperately to the last vestiges of prosperity that it had enjoyed before the dual carriageway had avoided it and a new Tescos had dragged the shoppers and reluctantly the shops to the other side of town. It now lay marooned, abandoned as if in a rush to avoid some catastrophe, surviving only at night in a half-lit world of Chinese takeaways and taxi cabs, chip shops and tattered pubs.

Mike stopped the car at the corner of Windsor Road and Queen Street.

'Alright here, boys?'

'Yeh, fine. Thanks a lot, Mike.'

Lewis and Daz climbed eagerly out of the car. Lewis turned to Mike before he shut the door.

'Thanks again, Mike. We'll see you on Saturday.'

'Aye, see you Saturday. It should be a good night.'

'It'll be a good laugh, Mike, but don't tell the wife.'

'You can be sure of that, Daz,' replied Mike a little too seriously.

Lewis closed the door as the car pulled away, isolating them outside the Cambrian pub. They immediately crossed Windsor Road. The drizzle had not abated. It sustained a veneer of water upon the smooth tarmacadam which shone in the reflected light of the shop and street lights. Every third car was now a cab and they stepped around one as it disgorged its three female passengers onto the pavement. Lewis smiled at one of the girls as he walked past. She, half-hiding under her hastily erected umbrella, half-smiled back.

'Know her, Lew?'

'Sort of, Daz. You know how it is, one drunken evening.'

They continued along Windsor Road, avoiding the bus queue, which stretched to two people, and the umbrellas which came swivelling towards them. Hiding from the rain. Everyone was in a hurry; get inside; get off the streets.

Immediately before the Kentucky Fried Chicken Shop, they turned down a narrow alley which led through a tunnel under a railway line to a small square lined by two pubs on the other side. The tunnel under the line lent its name to one of the pubs, the only one worth going to.

'Hell, Lew, there's a fucking queue. We'll get bastard soaked.'

Lewis didn't reply. They both continued walking towards the offending queue. A large man standing squarely in the doorway of the pub peered along the twisting line of heads, surveying it carefully for any possible miscreants. Having satisfied himself there was no immediate need to exert his presence on the plebs waiting to get in, he allowed three girls at the front to squeeze past him through the doorway. He then retreated into his citadel, abandoning the remaining clamouring masses to the drizzled sodium darkness of Market Road.

Daz maintained a constant exposition on the disadvantages of waiting in pub queues, referring to the indignity of it all, suggesting alternative venues and affirming the dampness of the rain. But both of them waited, shoulders hunched and collars turned up, making no effort to move other than towards the front and inclusion into the evening. Despite their reluctance there was a realism which prevented them from leaving. If they didn't get in their options were hopeless. They might as well go home.

'Two minutes, boys,' offered the bouncer in an ill-fitting dinner suit, before once more closing the door on their immediate aspirations.

'Fuck, I hate this queuing. Every weekend it's the same down 'ere.'

Lewis didn't reply. He was enduring the ignominy of the queue in the hope that it would be worth the wait.

Finally a face appeared briefly at the door before it opened allowing an escape from the crowd. They gratefully accepted the warmth and noise of the pub. The strain of the queue was instantly forgotten until they were next engulfed in it.

'My round, Lew. See if you can get us a table.'

'Aye, no problem, Daz. Do you want a foot stool as well?' replied Lewis as they attempted to manoeuvre towards the general direction of the bar. Lewis couldn't even see the barmaids behind the three strong crush at the bar, never mind find a spare table. He strained through the gloom and vaguely familiar faces to find someone he knew. Recognition eluded him.

He disliked the first seconds on entering a pub as a sea of faces rushed towards him, pressing for recognition, daring an isolation. His usual recourse was to dive for the bar, smiling inanely unless someone approached him directly. The crowd would soon confer an obscurity before it isolated the next entrant.

Daz appeared at his side with two pints of lager.

'Cheers, Daz.'

They both drank quickly. The pleasure of alcohol again after a break of thirty minutes was enlivening. The taste trickled to the mind, loosening.

'Crowded tonight, Daz.'

'Aye, there's a fair few in.'

They exchanged a few more platitudes before Daz started the real conversation.

'Seeing much of that girl you were with the weekend before last, Lew?'

'No, not really. I've tapped off with her a few times, but nothing serious.' Lewis was keeping the mid-week meeting to himself.

'Good looking girl, mind, Lew.'

'Aye, not bad. She's a nice girl too but you've got to watch the nice girls or I'll end up like Mike on my own stag night.'

'Aye, he must be mad,' replied Daz, not noticing the deft

switch in conversation.

'I mean, doesn't he know what he's letting himself in for?' questioned Daz, with the conviction of a man who thought he knew exactly what Mike was letting himself in for.

'I'm sure he knows what he's doing. He's a few years older than us, mind.' There was a tone in Lewis's voice that suggested he envied Mike's imminent marriage.

'You watch, he'll regret it. Give him a year or two. They all do.'

'There must be something in it, though, Daz. After all, most people do it, don't they?'

'Aye, and most people regret it, I can tell you. My Mam and Dad split up when I was fifteen. I don't think they ever got on properly. They were always bloody arguing, usually over nothing. Used to drive me and my sister bloody spare. We were glad to get rid of the bastard.'

Lewis was thrown by the vehemence of Daz's reply. He could remember Daz in school at that time or rather the lack of him. Mitching constantly with teachers muttering about unstable parental backgrounds. He was unsure how to reply on what to Daz was obviously a favourite subject. He began to drain his pint as a diversion while he thought of a suitable response, but before he had finished Daz continued his informed discourse on the ills of matrimony. 'I tell you what an' all. You ask any of the married ones up the club an' hardly any of them have a good word to say about it, and half of them are either divorced or split up. Na, you can stick that for a laugh.'

Lewis attempted to think of an instance that would contradict Daz's monopoly of the argument but Daz continued enthusiastically. 'Give them six months and they can't wait to get away from the wife. Stag night, birthday, tour: any occasion for a fucking few nights away. You watch the bus to Swansea Saturday night. It'll be fucking packed and half of the bastards will hardly know Mike.'

Lewis floundered under the basic accuracy of the argument.

'What about my boss, then? He's been married twenty-five years and he swears by it,' Lewis countered in an attempt to retrieve something from Daz's effective demolition of the merits of marriage. But Daz would not be dissuaded.

'Aye there's bound to be a few exceptions, but basically it doesn't work. All those hours cooped up with someone you hardly know at first and then when you get to know them they're nowhere near the person you thought they were. It's just plain lucky if you get on, but you're more likely to hate the sight of each other. No, you can bloody stuff the thing. I'll be fucked if I'm getting married.'

Daz paused from his bar oratory allowing Lewis time to finish his drink. Lewis hoped that Daz had finished with the subject. Faced with his obvious zeal he stood little chance of convincing him otherwise, especially over an issue he had little confidence in himself. He baled out. 'Another lager, Daz?'

'Aye.'

Lewis forced his way to the front of the bar. He always found it frustrating trying to order a pint in a crowded bar. It was a complicated technique requiring anticipation and split-second timing. Lewis didn't have it. The false calls were the worst, when he would order confidently for a round only to be completely ignored by the bar staff. It usually degenerated into a process of elimination with someone eventually responding to get rid of him.

'Two pints of lager, please,' he pleaded across the bar.

The bar, a simple device comprising a bare stand set up to facilitate the distribution of an expensive liquid, but also a feature that was the whole focus for countless evenings' entertainment. Lewis did not consider why he passed so much of his money across this two feet of intervention. He didn't even like the taste of the stuff. Was it a simple exchange-money for oblivion, the ability to forget? The tolerance he had developed served its limited purpose. He drank to get pissed. He was clear on that point. There were other benefits but they were incidental. He assumed his mates drank for similar reasons but there was a reticence to talk about it, sometimes an evasiveness. Perhaps some liked it, or preferred not to think about it. The prospect depressed him. Daz would agree with him but was always reluctant to pursue the topic to any conclusion: if there could be any. He said he preferred not to think about it. Lewis assumed he preferred not to talk about it.

Two pints of clear liquid appeared on the bar, forcing Lewis to hand over the required forfeit. Bubbles of carbon dioxide clung to the side of the glass, suggesting it had not been properly cleaned, while a punch of overspill swamped a sodden beer towel on the bar top. Standards were dropping but Lewis let it go. Two circles of alcohol momentarily appeared then disappeared as Lewis picked up the glasses and headed back into the crowd with his bounty to relocate Daz.

Daz was involved in a conversation with a man Lewis vaguely recognised. He acknowledged him with a brief smile as he stood uncomfortably waiting for an entrance into the discussion.

'Well I'll see you then, Daz.'

'Aye, I'll see you later.'

The man moved off into the crowd without acknowledging Lewis.

'Who's that, Daz?'

'He's from work, on the same gang as me usually. Plays football for the Oak. He's a bit of a grumpy bastard in the mornings but he's alright.'

Lewis didn't ask any further questions. His curiosity was sated. He could probably guess the rest: lived in a semi on a new estate; one wife to whom he was occasionally unfaithful; two kids both in school; drives a clapped out Cortina and drinks in the Wine Bar on a Sunday morning.

'Not much talent in 'ere tonight, is there, Lew?'

Lewis had a cursory glance around the pub. There were probably three men to every woman.

'There's enough,' replied Lewis with a confidently wry smile.

'Ark at you, right bloody Casanova.'

But Daz was smiling too. Lewis enjoyed some success with the women and Daz knew it. A broad boyish smile of white teeth coupled with a few calculated compliments usually achieved results.

'There's a girl over there looking at me now,' announced Lewis in confirmation of his optimistic outlook on the romantic possibilities.

'Sure,' replied Daz sceptically.

'Aye, she was in school with me.'

'Where?'

'Over there by that pillar. There's a group of them, the one in green.'

Daz studied the crowd.

'Bloody hell, Lew, you'd get arrested for that. She couldn't have been in school with you; she's never our age.'

'Well, she went to the same school as me. She was probably a few years younger but it was the same school.'

Daz laughed.

'Give over, Lew, try somebody a bit older, she's well past her bedtime.'

'I didn't say I was going to chat her up, did I? I just said she was looking at me.'

'Us,' corrected Daz. 'Anyway she was probably thinking what the fuck those two old bastards were doing here.'

Lewis did not reply, allowing a drinking silence to overtake them. The pub had absorbed yet more people, enticing them out and in on a dreary Thursday evening. There was no obvious source of attraction: a plain long bar; some unobtrusive town prints littering the wall. The video juke-box playing a separate song from the resident Thursday night disc jockey whose musical knowledge appeared to end just before the Sex Pistols. But the pub would be packed three or four nights a week with the young and soon to be married or the slightly older and divorced.

Lewis looked up at the video screen. A black female soul singer was apparently belting out an amazingly realistic impression of a Rod Stewart classic. The incongruity of it all appealed to him.

'Ay, there's Andrea over there,' announced Daz.

'Who?'

'You know Andrea, my cousin.'

Lewis followed Daz's gaze towards two women, one of whom he presumed was related to Daz as she had definitely smiled at one of them and Lewis certainly didn't know her.

'Who did you say she was?' checked Lewis.

'You know my cousin,' replied Daz, obviously assuming that Lewis had an extensive knowledge of his family tree. 'Well, second cousin anyway. Coming over to talk to her?'

'Aye, alright. What's her friend's name?'

'I'm not sure, Anna I think, she works with her.'

'Ok, you go over and introduce yourself and tell them how wonderful I am and I'll go and get another drink as otherwise we'll end up buying them one.'

'Aye, I'll tell them how bloody wonderful you are but don't be surprised if neither of them will talk to you when you come over.'

Lewis made his way yet again to the bar while Daz headed towards his cousin and her friend.

He was always keen to talk, anything to take his gaze off the video screen. It did not matter how much you detested the thing it still hung there demanding attention. But he disliked obviously approaching a stranger in a pub when he was sober. A friend's cousin provided an excellent non-threatening approach. He didn't like someone thinking he was blatantly chatting them up even when he was. He liked the look of Daz's cousin, but would he mind, considering she was a relative? But then he did say she was his second cousin: not that close, no problem.

As he approached the two girls, he realised they were older than he thought. Daz was talking volubly as they stood politely smiling.

'Here's my mate, Lew. Lewis, meet Andrea and Anwen.'

The two women smiled. Lewis smiled.

'Hi'ah.' He would have offered his hand but he was carrying the pints.

'Pleased to meet you.' He stumbled for another line but settled for a vague smile.

Lewis immediately lost interest in Andrea. From across the pub she had appeared attractive but looking at her now there was a harshness in her taut figure: no curves, only angles. Her eyes stretched her face into a grimace of a smile, an arid smile promising no warmth.

'So how come you're related to Daz here then?'

'Through marriage,' replied Andrea bluntly.

Lewis had a talent for banal opening lines.

'And you're cousins?' And he was too sober for any real charm.

Andrea didn't reply. The music was far too loud for conversation. A pub is designed to encourage drinking not talking. But the conversation stuttered along, obscured by smoke and muffled by the music. Lewis asked questions, Andrea answered them. Anwen smiled. Daz drank.

'So how do you two know each other then?' asked Lewis hoping to draw Anwen into the conversation.

'We work together,' replied Andrea.

'O'aye where's that then?'

'In the DVLC.'

Lewis scrambled for some mutual area of interest. 'It's something to do with car registrations, isn't it? I think I got mine from there.'

'Everyone gets them from there,' replied Andrea scornfully.

Lewis stumbled uncomfortably for a reply.

'C'mon And. It's hardly an exciting talking point,' admonished Anwen, rescuing Lewis from further embarrassment.

This was a development that Lewis had been hoping for. A chance to draw Anwen into the conversation. It was a circuitous route but it usually worked.

'Do you enjoy it?'

'It's okay, I suppose, but it can get a bit boring. There's not much variety in the bloody forms.'

'C'mon, they come in at least three different colours.'

'Four,' replied Anwen.

They both laughed.

Lewis now gave up on witty comments. He was concerned only with Anwen. Each question was designed to induce Anwen to talk, to reveal something of herself. She enjoyed the attention. She was several years older than Lewis. He remembered her vaguely from school: a tall goddess figure far removed from his world of football teams and Saturday nights in front of the tv. But now they were closer and tonight he wanted to be as close as she would let him. More lagers relaxed him and buoyed his confidence as the round with Daz continued. Daz became increasingly isolated with his cousin who began looking determinedly for someone else to enliven her evening.

Finding no one, she confronted Anwen.

'You ready then, An?'

Anwen turned to her, annoyance evident in her expression.

'It hardly seems worth it now. It's almost ten-thirty; by the time we get to the Cam it'll be nearly closed.'

'No, don't go now; you might as well stay. Me and Daz will walk you to the bus stop,' enthused Lewis. He was in now and he didn't want Daz's cousin to blow it just because he hadn't chatted her up.

Andrea stared fiercely at Anwen but didn't reply.

'Do you want another drink, Andrea?' asked Daz, blithely unaware of the seething anger surrounding his cousin.

'Well I thought you would never ask. I'll have a vodka and orange.'

'Anwen?'

'Martini and lemonade, please.'

Daz looked at Lewis.

'Lager.'

Daz trudged off to the ever-willing bar with the vague conception that he had missed something.

'So you're going to walk us to the bus stop, are you?'

questioned Anwen as she succinctly smiled at Lewis.

'Aye, if you'll let me,' Lewis replied confidently. He was on a roll now and he knew it. Each alcohol-lubricated phrase, relaxed in its assurance, slithered off his tongue.

'Well that's strange because I'm not catching a bus home, I'm walking, but you can walk me home if you want to.'

Her eyes promised more than a simple walk home and Lewis had difficulty in concealing his enthusiasm. In fact he wanted to start running.

'I thought you lived in Malci?' He was trying not to rush it.

'I do but it's at the bottom of the hill. It's easier to walk.'

Lewis considered the situation; of course it was easier to walk.

'What about you, Andrea?'

'Oh don't worry about me. I'm catching the bus,' replied Andrea sharply.

'Well we can walk you to the bus stop first.'

'No it's alright. I can find my own way there, thank you.'

Lewis abandoned the issue. He had offered but he didn't really care if she walked, caught the bus or flew home.

Daz appeared with the girls' drinks. Anwen thanked him, Andrea just accepted the vodka. He returned to the bar for the lagers, leaving Andrea to swiftly finish her drink while Lewis and Anwen indulged in understated laughter.

'Well I've got to catch the bus,' announced Andrea curtly. Anwen turned to her friend, unsurprised by her sudden wish to leave the pub.

'You don't have to go yet, And. Stay a few minutes and we'll walk with you to the bus station.'

'No thanks, I'm going to go now.'

'Are you sure?'

'Quite sure.'

'Same time in the morning then, And?'

'Yes, I'll be there.'

'Goodnight then, And.'

'Yes, see you again,' added Lewis.

But Andrea was already heading for the door.

'I think your friend is upset,' commented Lewis, making a supreme effort to sound and look concerned.

'She'll be alright in the morning. She gets jealous sometimes, that's all.'

'Of what?' enquired Lewis, feigning naivety.

'Of my hairstyle. What do you think she's jealous of, it's all the attention you've been giving me with precious little to her.'

Lewis smiled.

'Don't mind, do you?'

'No, I'm not complaining. She was just feeling a bit left out that's all,' explained Anwen in defence of her friend despite the sharp exit.

'Never mind, she's gone now. Shall we make a move?'

'What about your mate?' asked Anwen, obviously surprised at Lewis's willingness to abandon his friend.

'He's a big boy, he can look after himself.'

'Won't he mind?'

'No, of course not. It's almost stop-tap anyway.'

Daz re-emerged from the crowd balancing the drinks.

''Ere you are, Lew, grab this.'

Lewis relieved Daz of his extra pint.

'Where's Andrea gone?' asked Daz surprised at his cousin's sudden disappearance.

'She's gone home.'

Lewis swallowed large gulps of lager in an effort to finish his pint quickly.

'I thought we were going to walk her to the bus stop.'

'She's catching the earlier bus and Anwen is going to walk home,' replied Lewis after another substantial swallow of lager.

Anwen finished her Martini, then smiled at Lewis.

Lewis was leaving. 'Anyway we've got to go now,' he announced with an emphasis on the 'we' as he handed his glass to Daz. 'So I'll see you Saturday for the game.'

Daz looked at Lewis with the gaze of a man who was not really keeping up with events.

'Aye, alright, Lew, see you then. Nice seeing you, Anwen.'

'Goodnight,' murmured Anwen as she turned into the diminishing crowd.

Daz watched Lewis follow Anwen to the door. He was unsure where he had missed it all. As Lewis reached the doorway he turned around and with a broad smile winked at Daz before disappearing from view.

Lewis allowed Anwen to guide him through the town centre towards Malci. The town was as barren as a Sunday afternoon. The rain had stopped but the figures still hurried away, scuttling into the scattered darkness of shop displays and street lights. Throwaway food wrappers punctuated the pavements, sodden and disintegrating with the wetness. A pair of policemen walked passed them, peering suspiciously into piss-stained doorways and parked cars. People were scarce, scuttling shadows catching taxis or driving home. Not everyone drank on a Thursday night. The warm food-laden air of the Kentucky Fried Chicken Shop caught a number of indecisive stragglers willing to part with yet more unnecessary hard-earned money. Even, perhaps especially at night, the town centre was a money trap; the money spider spinning its hessian threads to slowly engulf and submerge the money spenders.

But Lewis was past spending for tonight. He knew the web, aware of its threads; he was retreating with the spoils.

Their conversation died as they walked through town, choked by the damp clinging air. It was now a rush to get inside again, to refuge, abandon the abandoned streets. Lewis sensed the atmosphere; he did not want to linger. On a clear night in summer he may have found her face in the stars. Being a romantic, he often went over the top. But tonight it was a straight walk to her flat. The talking could wait until later. He tentatively took her hand hoping she would clasp his in return. There was no resistance or surprise as they held hands and continued walking. Lewis only felt a surge of excitement of the promise in her warm hand.

They circled Victoria Gardens, past the old library and the new surgery, before turning up towards Malci. Lewis was hoping Anwen did not live too far up the hill. He hated Malci hill. He had walked up the damn thing too many times, it easily absorbed his drunken strength. It lay there menacingly, waiting, before it increased its length and gradient especially for him.

He tested his fears. 'Where exactly is your flat then?'

'Don't worry, it's not far up the hill. We take the next right.' Anwen was ahead of his thoughts.

They turned down Elm Avenue. All the trees were planes but Lewis let it pass. The lower part of Malci hill was an area of large avenues, mature cars and quiet trees. What one might call a stockbroker belt, if the town had any stockbrokers, which it didn't. Lewis had not been expecting this, being more used to the Wimpey Estate with the snapped saplings and battered escorts.

'Posh road this, An. I thought you said you didn't get paid much in the DVLC,' commented Lewis.

'It's not that posh, I can tell you. It's all sorts down 'ere, and it's only a flat.'

Anwen opened the gate to a double-fronted house, blatantly Victorian in design. A large Monkey Puzzle tree shielded it from the avenue, but could not hide its decayed obsolete grandeur. It could have been built by a prosperous solicitor on the turn of the century coal boom. He had been keen to emulate the town houses of Guildford from where he came before becoming marooned by a poor degree and a socially inept wife. His period of prosperity was brief; he lost a small fortune on a mining venture and a wife through diphtheria. The war finished him off and he died in the infirmary at Longford, an institution he had once given generously to. But the house had remained. He had left his mark even though it awaited decline into a series of bedsitters.

'Lovely house.'

'Is it?'

'Well, yes, I think so. Just look at the size of it, and the brickwork.'

Lewis admired the craftmanship of a builder hundred years dead. A life not even consigned to someone's memory. But the house still remained, a monument not even to a memory, of a ruined lawyer and a bachelor builder.

'Well, I suppose so,' agreed Anwen, but the house held nothing for her and it disappointed Lewis.

'Quiet now. I don't want to disturb the owners.'

'I thought you owned it?'

'I just own the flat at the back and not the whole thing.'

'Oh.'

'Quietly, this way.'

Lewis followed Anwen around the side of the house. She did not ask him if he wanted to come in. She assumed he did. He assumed she wanted him to. They climbed an iron fire-escape to a white door on the first floor. Anwen gently opened it as she re-emphasised her instruction.

'Please don't make much noise. I don't want the neighbours to know I've got a man in here.'

Lewis thought about asking what difference it made but he guessed what the neighbours would be like. He unconsciously tiptoed across the living room to a settee which offered a welcome refuge.It had been placed in worship to the television which dominated the flat from its own revered altar.

'Lovely flat, An,' complimented Lewis. He was struck by the space and intrigued by how she could afford it. Obviously the DVLC paid more than he realised.

'Yes, I like it. Coffee?'

'No thanks.'

'Tea?'

'No thanks.'

'Anything else?' called Anwen from the kitchen.

Don't be silly now Anwen, thought Lewis. Forget the drinks.

Just come and sit on the settee with me.

'Sure?'

'Yes, thanks, I've had enough to drink in the pub. Do you think I can use your toilet though?'

'It's through there.'

Lewis gratefully headed for the toilet. He'd been dying for a piss all the way back. He had considered several side streets but had decided he didn't know her well enough. It would not have helped.

When he returned to the living room, Anwen was sitting on the settee. Perhaps she was drinking the coffee she had made for herself. She smiled briefly at him as he sat down. Lewis hesitated for a few seconds before resolving to kiss her. Here was the crunch; he was rarely this wrong.

He wasn't this time.

They kissed assuredly, both knowing the game. The rules were complicated but once learned they were easy enough to remember. The noise of skin sticking and coming apart curdled through the room, their movements following the blithe rhythms of love songs on a compilation album. The songs all recalled the same theme following each other effortlessly: easy partners among lovers. It was the same game: in the end everyone lost.

Lewis knew the routine, every action designed for a response. Anwen played. He kissed; she used her tongue. He kissed her neck; she closed her eyes and sighed, tilting her head just enough to allow him to scour her neck. He had an erection by now, produced by the promise of sex. There was no thought to it; it was there. There was no way she could not have felt his dick as they lay entwined, slowly writhing on the settee.

Lewis ran his hands over her tits, pressing firmly on the expected areas. She gasped obligingly as his hands touched the bare skin exposed by the cut of her dress. He almost laughed. It couldn't have been that exciting. Memories of the previous night on the mountain with Louise played in his mind. He made a mental note that the girl's name was Anwen. It shouldn't have been difficult as they had few similarities. Anwen pulled his arse into her and he felt a few seconds of genuine excitement before the routine took over once more.

He attempted to slip the top of her dress off without much success until she assisted him, undoing her bra at the same time. He removed his T-shirt. Lewis looked at her tits as they flopped free; the different shape of nipples and breasts fascinated him. Anwen was not unusual: they were not odd in shape and the right one was definitely not nine degrees left of centre. They were different but then they always were. There was no embarrassment or intrusion of words as they rejoined naked from the waist up. They had both been here before, not with each other but it didn't matter. Lewis was about to undo his trousers when she began to do it for him. It was a struggle with the first button before eventual success released the others, allowing her hand to grasp his dick through his boxer shorts. Getting it out took longer; she eventually drew it through the hole in the front of them that he never used. He resolved to buy them holeless next time. He knew her hand was on his dick; it was exciting her hand was on his dick; but what was the feeling? Was there any touch? Perhaps it was because he was circumcised. I mean all that skin must have been designed to do something.

He was unconcerned when after a few brief squeezes and ill-directed tugs she abandoned it like a Christmas toy that had failed to perform as expected. Lewis at this time, still in auto-pilot, was kissing her nipples, nibbling them between his teeth as he coaxed them to raise fiercely from their flaccidity. He had once gone out with a girl whose nipples absolutely refused to erect to any form of stimulus. This was confusing as the girl would go into raptures at the first sign of a kiss with the most timid wandering tongue but with absolutely no impact on her nipples. Various incentives were anointed upon the unco-operative organs which although tasting more unusual remained resolutely inverted. He traced his fascination with nipples to this experience.

Their position didn't aid gentle caresses, only a rough frantic body groping. But then what can you expect. The settee became progressively cramped with moving bodies and strewn clothing. Lewis took a breather from kissing as she clasped him into her, this time with hands on bare skin. As he focused his eyes over her shoulder, relishing her nails as they turned predictably inwards he looked directly into the eyes of a tall crew-cutted man staring at him. The man held Anwen possessively in a recent photograph which stood so prominently on the coffee table that he really should have seen it before. But then he hadn't been looking, had he? A brief feeling of panic engulfed him before he dismissed it as an irrelevance. She couldn't be expecting the large short-haired gentleman back imminently. Surely she would have mentioned it? Oh, by the way, my psychotically possessive boyfriend/ husband is due off his shift at two but he sometimes finishes early. There was something in his eyes that suggested that he might be more than a little concerned to find that someone, namely Lewis, was trying to bonk his girlfriend on what was probably his settee.

'Er, Anwen,' murmured Lewis unsure where to begin.

'Yes,' she replied in a voice which promised everything or at least a blow job.

'Er, don't mind me asking but I was just wondering who, uum, the bloke in the picture is?'

'What picture?' her voice hadn't changed.

'This one by 'ere on the table.'

'Oh that's my fiancé.' There was still no change in tone. Obviously she was not unduly concerned.

'Oh, I see.'

Lewis began to kiss Anwen again. He was unsure whether to continue his interrogation or what approach to make. He could hardly storm off in indignation at broken promises as he hadn't exactly been forthcoming about personal information himself. But he did expect a certain complicity of motive; she could have at least moved the picture before they started kissing on the poor bloke's settee.

'Er, this might seem like a strange question. Don't think I'm prying or anything, but where is he at this precise moment?'

At this precise moment Anwen was down to a pair of knickers and Lewis had his trousers around his ankles with an erection almost up to his chin. He thought it was reasonable to determine the chances of meeting the short hair-cutted gentleman during the next hour or so.

'Don't worry, he's on his TA's annual outing.'

'Where to?' asked Lewis during a premonition of the tattooed giant returning prematurely from a week's sortie in the Brecon Beacons, unshaven, hungry and looking forward to bonking his girlfriend only to find Lewis had beaten him to it. An enemy he could identify more convincingly with than any false shadows he'd been chasing on a toy soldier's weekend in the Welsh hills.

'Amsterdam.'

Lewis began to relax.

'How long's he gone for then?' Increasingly unconcerned as he pulled Anwen's knickers over her hips and downwards.

'Just the weekend. That's why I didn't want to wake the neighbours. You know what they're like,' replied Anwen as she closed her legs enough to allow Lewis to remove her knickers.

'Do you think he'll mind?' asked Lewis as he stood up to kick his trousers off from around his ankles. There were always the ridiculous moments during screwing on a settee which made it all worthwhile.

'Oh yes, if he found out, but then I'll mind if I find out about all them whores he'll be shagging on his little trip to Amsterdam. There's not much basic training in Holland is there? Unless you like flowers and we haven't got a bloody garden.'

'Didn't you play hell about him going then?'

'The bastard told me they were going to Exmoor, but then he spent three hours last night looking for his passport. I knew where it was, but he couldn't ask me for it, could he?'

'Well not really, no.'

'I rang the bus company and they told me. Some bloody security. Anyway, are we going to get on with this or not?'

There was a note in her voice that suggested Anwen was losing patience with Lewis's questioning. Lewis could feel his erection deflating like a punctured balloon at a children's party. He looked at the picture of the part-time soldier scowling at him, blissfully unaware that his fiancé knew that he was really in a cheap hotel in Amsterdam and not bivouacking on Exmoor. Lewis vaguely recognised him; it was a small town. He'd seen him running around the pond. Lewis had a good memory for faces; he wished he could forget this one. He resisted slightly as Anwen continued kissing him; most balloons will reinflate if you blow hard enough. The picture scowled at him again. He smiled back.

FRIDAY

Lewis awoke to an insistent pressure on his shoulder, rocking him gently but purposefully.

'You'd better go, Lewis.'

'Uh.'

'It's getting light. You can't stay for breakfast; the neighbours will see you.'

'Breakfast? What?' Lewis's thoughts were engulfed in a mist of poor memory, before the realisation of where he was hit him like a bag of cement.

'Shit.'

'C'mon, you'll have to get up. It was a good night but keep it to yourself, please, love.'

'Aye, sure, Anwen.' He kissed her as he replied and smiled sadly. There was a note of desperation in her voice where she was hoping she could trust him but did not know for sure. He was aware for the first time of the gulf between their lives; she had a lot to lose here, he had a few teeth at most. He knew the rules.

'C'mon you'll have to go.'

'Aye, okay, my head is a bit zoned, that's all.'

Lewis had not drunk a large amount but his mind was far from clear. He was naked and he felt it. His mouth was what he imagined the inside of a coffin to taste like. He wanted to spit out the phlegm that adhered to his gums onto the carpet, but it would have bounced out into the living room. A mild hangover; a slight blurring of the senses.

He headed for the bathroom where he swilled his face, then his dick in sharp water from the sink. His dick shrivelled away in protest. Why hadn't it shrivelled away last night when he was thinking with it? But it had been a good night and at least there were no further commitments. He changed quickly in the half-light where Anwen had retrieved his clothes from the living room and placed them on the bed. He was fully clothed when she reappeared with a coffee in her hand, nakedness concealed by a white towelling dressing gown. He had a hard-on immediately, her accessibility exciting him. She remained defensively leaning against the doorway, her head bowed, not wishing to confront the reality of a man in her bedroom. Lewis stopped in front of her and she lifted her head dutifully to kiss him. She was still playing the game. Somehow her lips were warmer, softer after sleep. She prolonged the kiss but as he began to pull the dressing gown away from her legs she held his hand and pulled away. He realised it was the final play.

'You've got to go, Lewis.'

'Yes,' he smiled. 'Thank you, Anwen. It was a lovely night.'

In a moment he had let himself out of the flat, descended the iron fire-escape and crossed the tree-lined avenue, moving quickly in the direction of home. If he rushed he could just make breakfast. He laughed out loud as he recalled the night's events, startling a black and white cat which jumped off a red stone wall and scuttled away in the half-light of a reluctant dawn.

He passed his old school on the way home. Its gates padlocked by the janitor the evening before; a defence against the children. Children who throughout the day were desperate to leave it. Only hours after their afternoon release the unnaturally empty evening school would draw them into its deserted corridors and vacated classrooms to concentrate disorder where they would not concentrate during the day. A prominent sign warned that the school grounds were patrolled by security guards. Lewis laughed. He certainly hadn't seen any security guards on the occasion when, with an accomplice, he had broken into the school canteen in pursuit of a few dozen Mars bars and a pack of Fanta. He had been lucky that time and he knew it: not even an alarm never mind a raving alsation with a security guard in tow. The memory teased him; he could see its futility but did not regret it.

The school lay silent, an acropolis for his abandoned aspirations, its red brick walls turgid with decay. Thwarted ideals, disillusioned tearless teachers, all entombed within its vaults, entrapped in the drudgery of repetition.

He walked quickly on. The light from the street lamps fading, as the sun, frustrated by the heavy cloud bank which dominated the skyline to the east, grudgingly lit the morning.

Lewis arrived home to a black reproachful look from his mother. She did not ask where he'd been. She guessed; he did not dare dispute it. He quickly escaped the heat of the kitchen to change into his working clothes. He returned to eat his breakfast without speaking to his mother or father. The tension at the table was tangible. His mother shunned him for straying from the maternal home: into the arms of another woman. Or so he assumed. She never questioned Lewis on the nights he stayed out: just the black look of disgust. Lewis allowed her to fester in the fertile swamp of her own imagination. He didn't feel the need for explanation. He would only lie.

He escaped the impending kitchen inquisition, picking up his lunch box of sandwiches on the way out, smiling unsurely at his mother as he did so. Despite her disapproval of his imagined actions, she had prepared his sandwiches.

The two middle-aged commuters had caught their bus by the time Lewis arrived at the road to meet Roy. The sixth-former was still waiting for hers but again she preferred to look straight through Lewis, more interested in the weeds struggling through the cracks in the pavement. Lewis hoped the school holidays were not that far away, otherwise this apparition of academic beauty would damage his confidence irreparably. Hopefully by the time she resumed for the summer her present boyfriend would be an ex.

Royston's van pulled up and Lewis jumped into a welcoming smile from Roy.

'Looking a bit rough this morning. Out on the town last night?'

Lewis was used to his perception.

'Aye, stayed out a bit late.'

'Looks like you stayed out all night to me.'

Lewis acknowledged his guess.'May have Roy.'

'She any good, Lew?'

'Not bad. A few drawbacks though.'

'Married, was she?'

'Not exactly, but she was getting there.'

'Any chance of her husband finding out?'

'Fuck, I hope not.'

Roy laughed and returned some of his attention to driving. Lewis waited for the questioning to fade into the noise of the morning traffic.

'Hawkes's first. We've got to get the floor of the garage down today.'

Lewis allowed himself to become absorbed by the carbon monoxide warmth of the van. He needed the extra rest he would get from travelling to Hawkes's to pick up materials.

Roy cajoled his van through the traffic towards the builders merchants which lay on Ferry Road at the abandoned end of town. The van struggled over the steep flyover, reluctant to get to Hawkes's. Lewis was in no hurry either, but Hawkes would shake him out of his lethargy. They descended into the industrial estate beaconed by an expanding gas tower which acted as an unwelcome barometer of the town's prosperity. According to Roy, it had been on low pressure for the last twenty years. The industrial estate was a recent innovation (or at least the title was) conceived in a flurry of good but desperate intentions in the wake of mass lay-offs. The old industries burnt or worked out with a hundred years of exploitation. Nobody had put anything in during the last twenty years, except the workers who had given their lives. The people with the power taking government money and running in the face of nationalisation. Now the doctrine was privatisation and the government trickled more money into the industrial areas and, in the most neglected wastes, the enterprise zones. Ferry Road was a sporadic affair, planned half-heartedly knowing the big money would go to the towns further east. Consequently the big money had gone further east. Ferry Road was a shelter for a few small subsidiaries which had ventured an exploratory finger: aware that it was just as easy to remove it if the pie became too hot or the cake too small.

But Hawkes was a local man. He would have claimed that he had exploited the government: taking the grants and the loans to set up his business when he knew he was onto a winner anyway. He monopolised the building trade; there was no one else in town any more. One of the national firms had bought out a rival for him, but they had not understood the local area and their accountants had soon closed it down as the returns diminished while Hawkes had flourished. He drove his yard and his men obsessively hard. Everything had to be done at pace. He admonished the slightest mistake, cajoled the slow and sacked the lazy. It was said that half the building trade had worked for him at one time or another; few could stand the regime for long. It was run not as a builder's yard but a labour camp. The youth training scheme had refused to deal with him after one too many trainees had quit, citing abuse from Hawkes as a reason. He didn't care. He was making money, loads of it and it drove him on; the scent of it excited him. Now he could only see the balance sheets as the materials exited the yard as fast as he could get them in. The builders used him because he was cheap; he had all the big contracts. Roy used him because he liked him. Lewis enjoyed the free entertainment.

'I wonder what planet Hawkes is on this morning?' speculated Lewis, breaking the monoxide silence.

'Who knows? He can't slow down, that's his problem.'

Lewis looked at Roy to see if he was kidding. He wasn't. Lewis hadn't seen Roy slow down very often either.

As the van pulled into the builder's yard it was engulfed in a morass of activity. A lorry which had been delivering plasterboards had become stuck through the driver's attempts to execute a three-point turn when it would have been far easier to reverse out of the yard. Several small vans the size of Roy's were stuck waiting to load up with sand, while a forklift was edging back and forward, nervously balancing its cement-laden pallet.

Hawkes was furious. He was hanging onto the lorry's side-view mirror, bobbing manically up and down while shouting obscenities at the driver.

Lewis relished the scene. He was hoping for some entertainment but this would set the day off.

In his wild gyrations Hawkes's deerstalker hat had fallen off as he clambered around the front of the lorry, banging on the windscreen. The driver was having a torrid time grinding his gears desperately as he tried to locate reverse.

The occupants of the other vans were all enjoying the entertainment. It was all part of the attraction of Hawkes's builder's yard. Blunt and Hunter, the national outfit who had made a brief costly venture into town, could not have competed with this unless they employed a resident comedian and acrobat instead of a site manager. Hawkes's employees stood around nervously shuffling their feet in the spilled sand; obviously it was not such a good start to the day for them.

Eventually the harassed driver found reverse and in relief first. The lorry then accelerated out of the yard with Hawkes chasing it like a frenzied dog worrying a recalcitrant sheep.

The spectating vans, satisfied that the entertainment was over, dispersed into the corners of the yard. Roy waited his turn to pick up chippings and sand. Lewis had not stopped smiling when there was a tremendous slam into his door, as Hawkes thundered into it with his capped boots. Lewis should have remembered this was going to happen; it was a standard Hawkes routine.

'When the hell are you going to get a new van, Watkins?' opened Hawkes aggressively.

'When you give me some bloody discount in this place,' retorted Roy.

'What the fuck do you need a bloody discount for? You pinch half the stuff you carry out of 'ere anyway.'

'I need to fucking pinch it the prices you charge, and while you're at it get your daughter to fill them invoices in properly and I might pay the bastards. Half the time you're charging me for stuff I've never had; no wonder you make so much fucking money.'

'I don't know why I send you invoices. You take six months to pay the bastards. It's not Lloyds down 'ere, you know, it's a fucking builder's yard. Any more late payments and it'll be cash on the nail.'

'Ah fuck off, you don't know what a nail is and you're running the yard. Come out with me and do some real work for a change.'

'Ah bugger off. What you want, sand?'

'Aye, chuck 'alf a ton on.'

At this point Hawkes gave up exchanging abuse with Roy and ran across the yard in an exaggerated zig-zag pattern as if trying to avoid a sniper's bullet. He stooped successfully to pick up his hat on the run and then, pretending to pass it as if it was a rugby ball to one of his startled employees, side-stepped a stack of bricks.

'Get this man some sand,' he bellowed to no one in particular. A man in green overalls emerged from one of the signing out sheds and ambled purposefully towards the loader. But he was not quick enough for Hawkes, who by now was wound up into a frenzy of activity. He dived for the loader, pushing the slow but willing employee out of the way. He then accelerated sharply into a pile of sand, scooping up the required amount before reversing frantically backwards, scattering the men on the yard. Lewis felt the suspension shudder as the sand thudded onto the back of the van.

'Want some chippings, Watkins?'

'Aye, same again and watch the paintwork.'

The same manoeuvres were now repeated with the chippings. The loading yard had now cleared to avoid Hawkes's erratic driving.

'Anything else?'

'Aye, a discount on six bags of cement and a date with your girlfriend.'

'You can have the girlfriend but the cement is full price.'

'Boys, six bags of cement for Mr.Watkins here.'

Two workers ran to carry the cement to Roy's van. Lewis was watching and listening to everything in fascination. He had seen most of the antics and the line about the girlfriend was a regular, but he always enjoyed a good film even if he had watched it before.

'Don't forget to book the bastards out this time,' shouted Hawkes as a final retort as he disappeared into a large storage shed to recover from his exhausting performance.

'Five minutes, Lew. Just book them out.'

Lewis watched the yard return to an uneasy normality. It never completely relaxed, there was always an awareness of a fragile calm. There was something dangerous about the place. The boss.

Roy disappeared into the office; Lewis returned his gaze inwards, ignoring the yard. Images of the night before seeped into his mind: the easy laughing chat-up he had performed in the pub and the short walk home not even filled with promises. The unquestioning need for sex in Lambert's smell of dog. The need to have sex at that moment becomes all consuming, its pungent scent drifting into an obsessed mind. There is no alternative once that point has been reached; the need reduced to the basic task of penetration. Get wet, get in. Any utterances, any subterfuge becomes acceptable. The senses take over as we become animals of instinct, creatures of procreation in a world where you can fuck anyone. But now.

By the time she had revealed that she shared the flat with her boyfriend Lewis was too far in. He doubted if it would have made any difference earlier. He struggled to avoid his own stagnant conclusions. It was the same feeling of disgust that had engulfed him when he had finally come inside her: the abhorrence of physical contact at that moment; the need to be released; the feeling that still occupied his mind as she caressed him in disappointment, hoping for more. It would be twenty minutes before he tried again.

The driver's door scraped open and Roy climbed in, releasing Lewis from the discourse with himself.

'Right then, Lew, I want this garage floor finished by lunchtime. Job an'finish.'

Lewis smiled. He had worked Roy's job an'finishes before. He rarely finished any earlier and he recalled one occasion when he was still digging footings into the yellow clay at seven-thirty. But on the face of it this was a job an'finish with potential. They could just scrape away by three. Most builders knocked off at one on Friday and then it was down the pub for a few swift pints before the serious drinking started. But not Roy. Lewis often found himself driving into the yard late on a Friday afternoon, when even Hawkes had slowed down, for a bag of cement to finish a wall or a lintel to hold up a house. The afternoon drinking he didn't mind missing. It was the extra time to himself he could have used: to read the paper he rarely had time for during the week or even a walk around town smiling at the shop assistants.

'Aye, okay, Roy. We'll have a go at it. I could do with the afternoon off.'

'Right then, you just keep the bankers coming and I'll lay the stuff.'

The engine complained vociferously about the extra weight

as Roy coaxed the van out of the yard. They laboured once more through the traffic and out onto the dual which cut a swathe across the low-lying marshland to the south of the town. They turned off before the dual grafted itself onto the motorway. The road climbed upwards through a narrow valley to Longford and the site of their repetitive exertions for the next endless shortened day.

It was past nine when they arrived at the site. Roy reversed the van down the alley at the back of the house, leaving Lewis to move the sand and chippings off the back into a pile within shovelling distance of the mixer, which stood in glutinous silence waiting for its rotational day to begin.

'Floor ready for the concrete, Lew?'

'Aye, Roy, I fixed it up yesterday. May need some levelling on the far side though.'

Lewis had prepared the garage for concrete with a base of shattered breeze-blocks, broken lintels and hardcore from the quarry. It was enclosed by a surround of breeze-blocks to a height of four inches. It has to be roughly level if you're ever intending to lay a garage floor. Lewis was unsure about the far corner.

'Aye, it's alright, Lew. Give us a hand with the polythene,will you.' Don't forget the polythene, it's important.

Lewis finished filling the mixer with a diesel substitute and helped Roy lay a heavy duty plastic sheet which would act as a damp course for the garage floor.

'Right then, Lew. Let's get going or we'll be back in the morning.'

Lewis returned to the mixer, started it at the second attempt and began to shovel. He worked on a ratio, one bucket of water, six of sand, three of chippings and one of cement. Ratios are important. Each banker would would take three such ratios with a variable amount of water. The banker would then fill the wheelbarrow three times: which he wheeled across the alley and into the garden where the garage was being built. It was important to get into a rhythm, shovelling wheeling, shovelling wheeling, allowing for no rest. Thoughts, however, were free to travel untrammelled as the body switched into automatic. Lewis quickly became the automaton as his thoughts churned through his mind.

The clean slice of a shovel through sand was now punctuated by the hard scrape of metal grating on the limestone chippings, which would give the cement its strength, turning it to concrete.

Lewis slipped easily into the ritual of work, his arms flexing as he drove the shovel into the mound of mixed sand and chippings. His back bending, attuned to the motion: the final thrust of the shovel into the mouth of the mixer. Its appetite never sated. He had to ensure that the mix was of the right consistency: not too wet or too stiff. But this came easily to him now. The routine of work had engulfed him.

'Right you are then, Lew, we'll have it now.'

Roy had finished trimming the edges of the polythene and was ready to begin setting the floor. Lewis tipped a third of the mix into the wheelbarrow; concrete spilled onto the sand-scattered floor as the mix quickly filled the barrow. He pushed the wheelbarrow along a series of two-by-six planks which served to stop the wheels getting stuck in the thick clay-saturated mud which engulfed every building site he had worked on. It was a boulder clay: a remnant from the last glaciers which had gorged their way through the valley a mere thirty thousand years before, smothering it in a thick glutinous clay. Once you were through the first two feet of top soil you hit clay. Lewis had dug and shovelled this clay into countless skips and wheelbarrows, the ochreous oxides staining his hands and clothes. In summer it drained slightly, making the work easier, but the clay lattices, always jealous of their hold, sucked in fluid and during the winter became completely saturated with absorbed water, even more reluctant to relinquish their wetness.

Lewis tipped the mix onto the polythene base of the proposed garage floor.

'A bit strong, Lew. Not so much cement.'

Lewis looked at the mix. It looked perfect to him. He didn't reply to Roy: just pushed the wheelbarrow back to the mixer. He was physically absorbed now; he didn't need to talk; he had set himself a goal of an early finish. His mind was in other places.

There was a night of arid sex upon a cramped settee. It intrigued him why she hadn't taken him into the bedroom for the first time. Was it too much of an intrusion into her other life? He was so used to settees and living room floors he had forgotten what it was like to have sex in a real bed without a hard carpet burning his knees. There was a time of long stolen afternoons with Marianne on her parents' bed, light filtering through the venetian blinds, the digital bedside clock warning of time lost never to be taken again. The obsession with time; knowing it was stolen time, time not really theirs, time remembered not savoured.

He kicked his mind away from the still too near thoughts. In desperation the morning scene at Hawkes's yard rescued him. Hawkes's exuberant, comic angry face forced him to smile. Did Hawkes really enjoy making money that way? Bullying his employees; entertaining his customers. Lewis didn't really care he was killing time. He had once asked Roy why he had never expanded his business, always only a two-man affair.

Others craved for more influence, a bigger operation, more money. Mortgaging themselves beyond sanity, running frenzied into a well paid for cremation. He had never received a coherent answer. Roy had mumbled about the futility of it all. Lewis presumed he didn't have the drive to expand, but then again he just might have been happy as he was. He made a good living, owned his own house and took a fortnight's holiday to the Med every year. No, it wasn't the lack of drive: he worked hard when he had to, rushing to fill a job in order for someone to cook in their own kitchen or if the tea was tasteless. But never for the money.

Lewis continued wheeling the barrow: throwing in the

ratios, everything repetition; from before. The mixer gathered his thoughts.

Daz appeared: a bemused face abandoned in the pub to his beer and a solitary walk home. He wouldn't take offence, they knew each other too well. They had been friends since the fifth form when they aborted school at roughly the same time. He had a clear idea of Daz's reasons: a fierce break-up between his parents, blame apportioned liberally and Daz hadn't escaped his perceived share. Lewis would have been surprised if Daz had anything but a vague idea of his own reasons for leaving. He had many shared memories with Daz but not that one: the summer of the green Mini Estate; the summer of dislocation from Marianne; a many handed car they had bought jointly from a friend of Daz's second cousin. They had driven it illegally around the mountain road where Louise had spoiled his Wednesday night. They had bought sunglasses and attempted to grow stubble in a futile bid to look older. Lewis drove it manically around the narrow country lanes, scaring docile cows in sun-hardened fields which had strayed too close to the walled road. The car back-fired generously and, like every car Lewis subsequently owned, poured copious amounts of carbon monoxide into the driver and passengers. His mother had been concerned that he might be taking drugs that summer; glue sniffing was still a Saturday afternoon out for the stupid. His eyes were wide but it was the monoxide. His mother would have been more worried if she had known the truth. They were lucky they didn't kill anybody. They were even luckier they didn't kill themselves. To finance the car they siphoned petrol from a removal van which was parked most weekends at the far end of Daz's road where the street lights ended and the fields encroached on the council estate. Anderson's removal van didn't possess a lock on its petrol cap and as a forfeit paid for the summer's miles.

The Mini and the summer came to a brief conclusive end when Lewis failed to turn on a sharp left hand bend and hurtled through a fence into a field beyond. This would have been fine in itself. The car was basically undamaged, the frail fence leaving little impression on the robust Mini. But as Lewis, struggling with laughter, attempted to reverse out, a blue and white car with a light on its roof blocked their exit. The police had been taking notes on an Allegro that had been burnt out the previous night. They were more than delighted to deal with an underage reckless driver. They tried to connect them with the Allegro but Lewis and Daz were too sharp for that. Daz had three points on his licence, Lewis seven. They also had to pay the farmer fifteen pounds each for the fence. He promptly put it back undamaged. They sold the car for scrap to pay the bills.

Lewis laughed aloud at the memory, startling himself back into reality. He was annoyed to find he was still mixing concrete. He searched for more thoughts to let his mind away. His body could stay mixing but he didn't have to be part of it. The motion of his muscles continued, absorbed by the rhythm, fatigue waiting but unlikely to get its chance. Waiting.

Saturday's game confronted him. It was the last chance to avoid relegation. Dunvant were top of the league; the club were one from bottom. It was a home game so there was some advantage there and with some luck and a wet day perhaps they could scrape a win. He hoped Daz brought his kicking boots with him as they would need a few extra points. Daz practised fanatically at his kicking but on match days he frequently went to pieces. The crowd, even the small one that watched the club, was enough to smother his confidence.

Lewis emptied the sixth banker into the wheelbarrow and cut the mixer. It slowly stiffened to a halt, allowing silence to engulf the site. The sounds of the morning were now able to reassert themselves. He poured the mix from the barrow into the burgeoning garage floor. They were a third of the way through; it would be an early finish.

'Put the tea on, Lew.'

Lewis didn't reply as he retrieved the radio from the van. It would provide a background noise as they digested the morning. He pulled a jumper over his head as he sat down; it had been a hard morning and he was sweating. He didn't want to get cold while he was resting as it would be harder to find the rhythm again. Roy joined him. He was usually second to sit down and take his breakfast as it meant leaving the job in hand. Lewis suspected he didn't bother when he was on his own, perhaps only taking a cup of tea from his flask.

The first few minutes were filled with the silence of the radio. Lewis ate most of his sandwiches; he wasn't counting on eating lunch today. He would work straight through if he had to. He wanted the afternoon to himself.

'Hawkes was playing up this morning,' commented Lewis, unusually opening the conversation for the morning.

'Aye, he's good value for money, but he's going to give himself a heart-attack at that rate.'

'You reckon?'

'Aye, the place is going to kill him.'

'He's making the money though,' Lewis offered as an excuse.

'Aye, he's making money, Lew, but what's he doing with it? What can you do with all that money anyway?' Roy asked the questions as if he was confident of the answers.

'I could think of a few things.'

'Aye, I'm sure you could. But what's he doing with it? He's certainly not working any less is he?'

'No but,' replied Lewis hesitantly.

'Well what would you do with it? You can't eat any more than you do. You're drinking to capacity. You wouldn't have enough to give up completely even if you could find something to occupy your time. You haven't got any family yet. What would you do with all that money?'

Lewis didn't reply. He was sure he could think of something to do with the money but for now it eluded him.

Roy continued. 'It's just that everybody's chasing it, and money hides itself very well. They've no idea what they're going to do with it when they find it, if they ever find it. Probably hanker after more. People have this vague idea that money will solve their problems if only they could have more.'

Lewis was now listening to his own as yet unformed opinions.

'I suppose it makes things easier.'

'Aye, I'll give you that. Everybody needs some money but they forget what they need it for. It corrupts people. It becomes a blind pursuit of wealth. Look at some of your mates up the club working for Eynons. They're working all the bloody hours going. What is it? Sixty, seventy hours a week? And what for? An extra few hundred quid. What are they going to do with it? They've no time to enjoy themselves. They're living to work.'

'Some of them need the money for the mortgage and the kids, Roy,' replied Lewis, attempting to justify the long hours.

'Fucking mortgages. It's just the banks prostituting people's lives. All those interest repayments, it's just greed that keeps them as high as they are. I know people need somewhere to live but the banks just screw you for thirty years and if you fuck up, "Oh I'm sorry didn't you read the rules?" And when you lose you really fucking lose, it's not only the board that's packed away at the end of the game, it's your life. Once they stop winning enough to satisfy their fucking shareholders, goodnight, thank you very much, don't bother playing again as your one throw's gone. Sorry, no false starts allowed. Didn't you read the rules?'

'Aye, but Roy, it's not explained to people; they don't think that hard about it.'

'Well they should. I've thought about it. What about you? How much of it are you going to blow this Saturday night pissing it up on that stag night? What game are you playing? Have you read the rules?'

Roy was angry, angry for himself and angry for Lewis still blindly playing. He knew what it was like to drink himself into the ground after a week of work.

'I'm going to have a couple of drinks, but it doesn't mean I'm pissing it all away. I've got a fair idea of the game, don't you worry. What's twenty quid anyway?'

'Have you, Lew?'

'Aye, I know what it is, Roy. Reality's shit all of the time; occasionally you need to lose it.'

'Why, Lew, what's wrong with reality? It's all you've got in the end, unless you take it really seriously and then you can throw the board away yourself. Reality's all you've got: this town, this job, your life. Isn't this job good enough for you? Do you think you're better than this?'

'What the fuck do you drink for then?' Lewis was angry and struggling with his ideas. Roy was goading him purposely, perhaps forcing him to try something he never had, perhaps forcing him to confront the fact that this was it; there was nothing else. But he couldn't see it through his anger.

'You know I've given up, Lew.'

'What's the matter? Can't take it any more?'

'No, I don't need it anymore. I know what unreality is all about. It's about thinking you're great, that all the women want you, and you're easily the toughest bastard in the place. But in the morning it's just you again, but with a stinking hangover to remind you that you weren't that good after all. The beer, Lew, it's a free ride but it's not free. Call it lager, bitter or some foreign shit with a strange name and a stupid bottle, it's all going the same way for the same effect, and they've got you. How often do you go into a pub and not drink? You'd feel almost naked. Once you drink one you want another one. You're not medically an alcoholic but who cares? There's no question of sobriety in this house. Just fill yourself with the fucking stuff until you go home. It's only swilling stuff anyway. You can't get really pissed blind drunk on it, can you? That would be useless for the fucking breweries; you wouldn't be able to stand up to buy any more drink. Stronger beer; more people fall over, less beer drunk; answer: weaken the beer. When was the last time you got really drunk, really pissed?'

Roy paused from his milkcrate sermon to take a swig of tea. Lewis thought he got that drunk every Saturday when he couldn't find a woman but then he did put a considerable amount of time and effort into it. Lewis allowed his anger to fade as he finished his tea and listened to Roy's words in his mind. He didn't feel like arguing any more. He stood up and returned to the mixer, starting it with a sharp turn of the cranking arm. He was determined to have the afternoon to himself. He submerged once more into the ritual of work.

The morning lengthened while a weak March sun struggled to reach its zenith above the cloud bank which still dominated the sky to the east and was now posting untidy battalions in advance of its approach. The sky has no shape in March, no definition: a blanket unmade on an unused bed.

The sun would not get much higher but he was grateful for it; it took him away and back, away from the sand and cement, back to the classrooms of his youth where he would sit impatiently waiting for the bell to release him, resenting the stolen hours taken away from him in mindless regurgitation. No attempt to kindle his interest, just copy this, take it home, keep it. We may ask you to pass an exam on it. The first years he had found difficult, the forced conformity, the urge to compete, the need to do well in the exams and please his parents. His results were reasonable, above average nothing special. Despite the meaningless of it all, the empty schoolyards and overfilled exercise books, he resolved to persevere, stick the fifth form out in the hope that the new sixth form college proposed would be less inhibiting. He could choose his own subjects and cut the rubbish: there would be less hours. Marianne would be there. He could see her without some pervert teacher telling them off for public affection. But then there was Mr Marshall and no Marianne. It was on a March day similar to the one that now turned his thoughts that Lewis had finally walked out of the school. He would return only for his art exam; Falstaff deserved that. He had believed him. The exam was a work of hate, nothing else, naked hate with no hidden nuances. He was surprised that he passed it. The examiners must have liked something. Perhaps it was the hatred; perhaps it was their own fear. They could see the distressed faces staring hopelessly out of a high dark school window into a blackness lit only by a weak March sun. Perhaps they saw themselves.

The sun was two hours past its highest point but still a winter low when Lewis closed the sound of the mixer for the final time over another week. The work had proceeded quickly; the floor was full. Lewis watched as Roy levelled it with a long straight edge: the wood pulling the concrete flat; individual chippings vanishing into the film of water, sand and cement. Lewis had watched the process many times but it still held a fascination: a craftsman at work, the firm sureness of the controlled powerful motions. And he was only pulling a garage floor straight. Lewis had tried to emulate Roy's adeptness at bricklaying but without any real style: the subtle flip of the cement from the trowel to the brick; the brick placed casually in position, adjusted with the base of the trowel; next brick. The speed was a skill of necessity Roy had developed when he was working with a gang for a few years after finishing his apprenticeship. They were paid per thousand bricks so you had to keep up with the rest of the gang to earn your way. With a good gang you were on big money but Roy had chucked it after a couple of years despite the better wages to crack out on his own.

Lewis occasionally thought about setting out on his own but invariably postponed making a decision about it despite encouragement from his father. There was a plethora of excuses he could possibly use and often did to justify his decision but the truth was he didn't want to tell Roy he was setting up on his own. There was a possibility which he didn't want to acknowledge that he would miss Roy. The job suited him to a certain extent; it was only him and Roy. Nobody told Roy what to do and Roy rarely came over the boss with Lewis.

'Oi, Royston, don't you ever stop work? This poor boy's waiting to get down the pub on a Friday afternoon. You're too old for it now, boy bach, but he's not.'

Royston and Lewis turned around to greet the welcoming

face of Walter Davies. He was leaning on a stick, grinning toothlessly at them while a black and white collie shepherded shadows around his legs. A flat cap flattened his features and covered his few remaining hairs from the wind and the rain or anything else that threatened to remove them.

'Haven't they buried you yet, Walt? I'm sure I saw your name in the dispatched column last Tuesday.'

'I'll out run you yet, Royston, never you fear.'

'Where've you been then? We thought you'd deserted us.'

'I haven't been able to get up here this week. The Mrs has been bard all week.'

'Oh I'm sorry to hear that Walter. Give my regards.' Royston had immediately lost his mood of abusive banter.

'Ah, don't worry about her. It's only a bit of indigestion, just wants to see that new black doctor down the health clinic if you ask me. 'Arf the women in the village seem to have something wrong with them at the moment. You should see the clinic. It's roofed.'

Walter enjoyed his good-natured afternoon slanging matches with Royston and he wasn't going to let something as trivial as his wife's indigestion spoil it. Especially as he hadn't been able to get out all week save for rushing back and forth to the chemists for various bottles of pills.

'Oh that's alright then.' Roy was also relieved at the apparently trivial nature of Mrs. Davies's illness as he looked forward to his chats with Walter. After the initial jocular exchange, Walter would often stand and watch him work and they would talk. He was kept up to date on the village gossip, the local rugby scores, the recently deceased and occasionally Walter would talk about Royston's father. They were contemporaries, knocking about the same pubs with the same women at the same time. Roy's memory of his father was now but a smiling photograph. Lewis liked to listen to these conversations when he had the opportunity. He could almost hear Roy listening, intent on absorbing all the information he could on a father he had only briefly known. Walter was a tangible link, someone who had known his father as a real person. Someone who had laughed, drunk with him, known him.

'You've just caught us, Walt. We're just about finished.'

'Not like you to finish at two on a Friday afternoon, Royston.'

'No, I know, but it's a job an'finish and I think we've been working the boy too hard this week.'

They both looked at Lewis for a response.

'I'm the only one doing any work around 'ere anyway.' It was a bold response and his audience laughed accordingly.

'Ay, you tell him, son. He's not working hard enough. In my day I used to be up to head height before lunch and I'd put a floor like this down before breakfast.'

'Aye, and when was your day, Walter? I'm sure you were a labourer on the castle and they put that up in the Middle Ages.'

'Never you mind. There's plenty of years left in me yet. I could still show you a thing or two about the building game.'

'You sure about that, Walter? I'm sure there's a plot booked up in the village cemetery with your name on it. Won't be long before you're kicking up the daisies.'

'Don't you worry about my plot. I know exactly where I'm going and it won't be through any pearly gates, I can tell you.'

Roy and Lewis both laughed at his honesty. It was well known that Walt was what was termed a bit of a boy.

'What you been up to then, Walter? I hear you've been popping over to see that Mrs. Fisher, you randy old bastard. Her husband's not cold in the ground yet, mun.'

'Never you mind, I can still turn it on when I want to, and if old George managed to stay warm during that frost in January he's been wasting his money on coal all these years.'

'You'll be needing a monkey wrench to turn it on soon, Mrs.Fisher or not.'

They both laughed and realised it was the end of the insults for another week. Walter usually commented on the state of Roy's latest endeavours but there was not much you could say about a garage floor; it was a garage floor.

'You've been hanging around this site for a while now, Royston. How many more weeks, do you reckon?'

'Another three, perhaps four. I've got to finish this garage next week and then the paths. After that it's mainly indoor work, tidying up a bit.'

'Dragged it out though, haven't you?'

'Aye, it was that spell of bad weather which set us back a few weeks. Ground was too hard to dig for days and then mud everywhere. And the tea's bloody awful when we get it. It'll be good to get away from here, won't it, Lew?'

'Aye, it'll make a change, Roy.'

'Where're you going next, Royston?' enquired Walter in order that he could re-route his walk.

'Well I think we've got a roof to put on down in Eleanor Street, by the park. If the damned woman can make her mind up.'

'I hope it's better than your last roof, Royston bach. Me and old Sam 'ere were almost seasick walking up the hill looking at the slates you threw on.'

'Don't give us that. It's your eyes. They've long gone, you're just too stubborn to wear glasses.'

Walter laughed.

'Do you know? I still haven't been paid for that job. I'm sure the bloody woman thinks I'm a lending service. I've laid out ten thousand putting the damn thing on and they're refusing to pay until I fix some bloody guttering around the back. I said give me the cheque and I'll be up straight away but they're insisting on the guttering first. They've got me over a barrel, see. If I don't go up there and tow the line I'm paying a fortune on my overdraft while they're only getting some extra water on their backyard.'

'You know what you should do then, Royston: get your bloody solicitor onto them.'

'It's not worth it, mun, Walt. By the time he shifts his arse and writes a letter, that's hundred quid. I can fix the troughing for that. No, it's not the money, it's the principle that annoys me. I've done all the work, even put on a few extras free and they don't trust me over hundred fucking quid. Well I'm going to send Lew up to fix it; I don't want any more to do with them.'

Lewis hadn't liked the pair withholding the money from the start. The woman's lover was always asking blatantly basic questions on the work as if he was some kind of building inspector. He had even asked if they had put the felt on before the slates. Of course not, we were going to put it on afterwards to keep them from getting wet. He was not looking forward to the guttering job that Roy had so generously entrusted to him.

'Anyway, Walter, enough of work for now. Lewis wants his job an'finish and at this rate we'll never get away.'

'Don't let me stop you, boys. I've got to get going. Anyway, I expect you'll want a few pints.'

'Sure you don't want a lift across to the village, Walt?'

'No thanks, Royston. This dog's getting lazier as it gets older. We're going to walk over to the Grange and then down past the pond to the village. I'm sure the rain will hold off until the afternoon.'

'Right you are then, Walter, see you next week. Look after yourself and say hello to Mrs. Davies for me.'

'Aye, see you then boys, and watch he doesn't work you too hard, Lew.'

'Aye, I will, see you, Walt.'

Walter turned and followed by his shadow walked around the side of the house turning up the road towards the Grange.

'Ready then, Lew?'

'Aye, Roy.'

'Cleared everything away?'

'Aye.'

'Washed the mixer out?'

'Aye.'

'Put the tools in the van?'

'All in.'

'Right then, let's get home, is it? It's been a long week.'

Lewis was relieved to see Walter disappear towards the Grange. He liked Walter and enjoyed the banter between him and Roy but at two-thirty on a Friday afternoon he was worried that his job an'finish was going to disappear in a cloud of conversation.

'He's 'ell of a boy Walt, in' he?'

'Aye, he's sharp with his tongue, old Walt.'

'Was he much of a bricky, Roy?'

'He wasn't bad, Lew, made a living, but he could never get around to making the break and working for himself, even though he was always threatening to.'

'Why was that, Roy?'

'Oh I'm not sure, Lew. Some people prefer working for a firm, takes the pressure away. You only have to put the hours in and you pick up the paypacket on Friday afternoon. No problems with people not paying over hundred quid of guttering.' Roy smiled ruefully to himself.

They were now rolling down the valley towards the dual carriageway and the short drive home through the desperate to finish Friday traffic.

'Why did you go self-employed then?' asked Lewis.

Roy didn't answer immediately. He just appeared to concentrate on the stuttering motion of the windscreen wipers. The rain that Walter had hoped would hold off was coming in with the tide flooding up the estuary. Lewis didn't think he would get an answer when Roy spoke.

'I'm not sure really. A number of reasons. I suppose I'd just had enough of what I was doing.'

'I've heard it was a good crack in the oilworks. The rates were good, weren't they?'

'The rates were good aye, and I suppose there were a tidy bunch of lads there. I was even in the works team. But it was the monotony that was finishing me. I was just laying bricks building those great ugly chimneys.'

'The ones they blew up last summer?' asked Lewis.

'Aye, that's right, ugly bastard things when we first built

them. It was what I would imagine working on a production to be like: brick after bloody brick, no room for any creativity. I'd have gone nuts if I'd worked there any longer. I don't know how these people punching holes in plastic survive on the enterprise zones. No wonder everyone's had it by the time they get home. You can't do anything after a day of that; just sit in front of the tv, don't even listen, then go to bed. Tomorrow same thing, go to bed.'

'It's not exactly a work of art we're creating here, mind, Roy,' Lewis suggested doubtfully.

'I know that, but at least with a house or even an extension you've got room to think. Something that with luck someone will enjoy and appreciate. Even if they don't realise it's your own work. With line laying you've got no chance.'

Roy paused before continuing. 'And there's your own boss part of it. It's not as easy as people sometimes think, with the paperwork in the evenings, pricing and worrying where the next job is coming from. But in the end you are your own boss. No bugger's telling you what to do except the government and I generally leave them alone and they leave me alone. It's easier that way. Anyhow, what's this sudden interest in my working history? You thinking of leaving me?'

'No, just something I'd been thinking of, and talking about Walter reminded me.'

Lewis wished Roy was not always so perceptive but he was not ready to bring it out into the open yet. He had a fair idea of where his life was going but he was not sure if he wanted it there.

He turned away to look at the curtains of rain as they traversed the marsh, sweeping up towards the town hiding in the mouth of the valley. The van grudgingly allowed the use of third as Roy attempted to guide it down the slip road and onto the dual. The distance before the slip road became absorbed into the hard shoulder diminished rapidly before Roy was able to squeeze gratefully onto the inside lane.

Lewis looked away from the marsh only to find himself

staring into the back of a black hearse which engulfed the road immediately in front of them. He turned automatically and looked out of the back window; over the upturned wheelbarrow, shovels and assorted buckets the chauffeur of the chief mourner's car stared fiercely at them. The poor bloke who lay very dead in the honey stained coffin now had a funeral cortege which included a rundown builder's van.

'Shit, Roy, I think we're in the middle of a funeral procession.'

'I know that, Lew. I'm trying to get out of the bloody thing.'

Roy was looking desperately into his smudged sideview mirror, scanning the unbroken rush of traffic which blocked their escape into the outside lane and away from the funeral cortege.

'Come on, Roy. Get us the hell out of this. The car behind is flashing now.' There was an embarrassed panic in Lewis's voice.

'I can't, mun, Lew. We're only doing thirty-five and I can't get the speed up to get out into the outside lane. I think we're stuck here until the next junction.'

Lewis took a brief look at the long line of mourners' cars which the hearse and Roy's van led down the dual. He wondered what they were thinking. He returned his view to the hearse. He hoped he wasn't buried on a Friday afternoon with a builder's van in attendance.

The procession proceeded slowly up the dual towards town. Lewis could feel himself drawn into the occasion, the deathly expectancy of the town. The town that would absorb his energies for the next forty years before it would finally absorb him. What would be the sum of it all: a stone memorial; gold embossed letters on a captains board; some sired offspring; bequeathed possessions in fading memories.

'I just hope we don't know him, Roy.'

'Perhaps it's better if we do. At least we can say we turned up.'

They both relaxed into the procession until the next junction released them.

Lewis had showered quickly. The contented stillness of his mother's house in the afternoon usually relaxed him. On his occasional afternoons off he would sit in the warmth of the living room, play some favourite tapes and read. But today the silence ignored him. He couldn't enter it; he needed to be with people. A walk into town provided a route away. A well folded set of ten-pound notes sat heavily on the clock radio in his bedroom. They challenged him to buy something, perhaps a new shirt for Saturday night. He wanted to look smart for the stag-night. Swansea on a stag-night was always odds on for some women. He could have ventured to the pub where Daz's firm met, but he didn't like afternoon drinking and there was the game on Saturday.

He allowed the radio to play to the prospective burglars his mother hoped it would deter, vacating the house for the subdued excitement of a Friday afternoon in town. It was a short walk through familiar sights unnoticed in a rush of drizzle which dressed the town in the dull overcoat of late afternoon. A number of the street lamps were on early, announcing their intention through the gloom. Several of the shops were hesitating to shut for the day, weighing the advantages of staying open. Would it be worth it? But the isolated chain stores which had colonized the town remained resolutely available for the occasional intrepid customer not dissuaded by the rain. Lewis ducked into Burtons on the edge of Queen Street and George Place. Confident signs bullied the timid shopper with emblazoned information on the special offers available in the great last chance sale. Lewis fingered the sale items, mostly winter and summer lines you couldn't give away. Despite the reductions he couldn't bring himself to buy anything. He moved onto the new Spring clothes. Nothing really interested him; there was a half reasonable woollen jumper, but it was a shirt he was looking for. There was nothing there so he gazed at the other shoppers. The sale had not drawn a crowd. Two middle-aged women weighed down by shopping and life examined a rack of T shirts. Their unrealized boredom emanated in waves. A male shop assistant stood as rigid as the mannequins in the window. He had had enough of serving people for one lifetime. A young mother pushed a pram and dragged a toddler through the half-opened doors. The assistant didn't even turn around. His eyes were fixed on the clock on the far wall, which promised to tick another thirty minutes before his release. Two years ago he had been staring at another clock on another wall, waiting to be released to the world of work. Now it waited for his retirement. Lewis thought he recognised the girl pushing the pram but then convinced himself he did not. The rain formed maps on the plate windows. He considered if there was a map for him; perhaps if he could read it there was a way out. A movement in the corner of his vision attracted his attention. The video-camera in this shop shot the same movie every day.

The map on the window appeared to suggest escape, so he did. He walked down Queen Street towards the castle. As he passed Smiths he recognised a figure shielding under an umbrella peering into a shoe shop window. He couldn't see her face but her figure, never hidden under a dark blue skirt and a navy cardigan, was memorable. Suddenly there was interest in the town for Lewis. He didn't really want to lead her on but what was the harm in a little chat? Anyway, he fancied a cup of tea in the MC, but not alone.

She was still at the shoe shop when he reached her.

'Excuse me, miss. Mind if I share your umbrella? Mine's in the wash.'

The corniest openings are often the best.

Louise looked up into Lewis's beaming face.

'Oh, hello. What are you doing in town on a Friday afternoon?'

There was no point in Louise answering Lewis as he was already under the umbrella with her.

'I might ask you the same question.'

'I've got the afternoon off and I've come in to buy some shoes for Saturday night. What's your excuse?' There was no warmth in her voice; she was wary of Lewis after Wednesday night.

'Oh, same sort of thing, but I can't get them with a flat heel.'

Louise smiled encouragingly at Lewis.

'Going anywhere special?'

'Swansea, if you must know.'

'Just asking, that's all, I was hoping you'd like to come for a coffee with me.'

Louise said nothing but returned to looking in the shop window.

'You know what amazes me about this town,' announced Lewis, continuing before Louise had the chance to reply, 'it's the amount of shoe shops. There's six in this street alone. What do people do with all the shoes they buy?'

Lewis looked hopefully at Louise. Her reflection in the window was smiling.

'Coming then?'

'Yes, okay, where are we going to go?'

'The MC. It's just off the square.'

Lewis held the umbrella as they walked back up Queen Street towards the square.

'What would you like?' asked Lewis as he shook the umbrella to loosen the small spheres of rain before folding it away in the doorway of the cafe.

'Just a coffee, please.'

'Ok, I'll get them. See if you can find a seat.'

Louise enjoyed his humour. Apart from an old man engulfed in the smoke of cheap rollies the café was empty. Lewis peered behind the counter. Morrezzi sat engrossed in the pages of a worn *Sporting Life*, slurping occasionally from a mug of warm milky tea.

'Er, excuse me.'

Morrezzi looked reluctantly up from the paper, casting a disdainful look in Lewis's direction. The last race of the day was about to start on the portable tv that Morrezzi had tucked away out of view of the customers. He had ten pounds riding on it. He didn't want to serve Lewis.

He lethargically raised his sedentary frame from the chair and waddled over towards Lewis. He was not built for speed.

'Whad'you want?' The southern Italian accent was still strong. Lewis was used to Morrezzi's truculent manner. He just didn't understand how he made a fortune as a café owner using it. Perhaps he hadn't. Otherwise he would be back in some small town in the foot of the Appennines. Morrezzi's dream was a local bar in Lapino: an olive wood counter; joints of cured ham hanging by hooks from the beamed ceiling and a few regulars with whom to drink and argue football. As he ignored the Welsh drizzle and imagined the form of tired horses he knew it was only a dream.

'Two coffees, please, Morrezzi.'

'Ay, don't I know you?'

Morrezzi asked him this question every time he came in. He had thrown Lewis out on numerous occasions when he had haunted the café as an invaders-obsessed fourteen-year-old. Morrezzi had expanded the back of the café into a sort of amusement arcade with bandits and video machines. It deterred the regulars and the shoppers, but the money he lost on the food and drink he more than made up on the machines. It was the craze of the space invaders and Lewis had been a primary contributor to Morrezzi's profits. Short on pocket money but rich in ideas, Lewis had perpetrated a number of schemes to get more playing time for nothing. Until you mastered a game it was expensive to play. Consequently he had developed a technique of flicking ten-pence pieces into the fifty-pence slot. You could also run up credits by switching the machines rapidly on and off at the plug. Morrezzi had eventually tumbled the scheme as the preponderance of ten-pence pieces supplemented by a generous helping of foreign coins began to dominate the fifties compartment. He caught Lewis in the act and summarily banned him for life. In reality this meant about a fortnight and, having served his sentence, Lewis extracted his revenge with a stolen magnet from the physics laboratory. The machines' microchips didn't enjoy the proximity of a magnetic field and Morrezzi was faced with a hefty repair bill.

'You been fiddling my machines again?'

'I'm too old for all that, mun, Morrezzi. Anyway, you've only got that old bandit left and when's the last time that paid out?'

Morrezzi smiled grimly, took the money for the coffees and ambled back to catch his latest losing horse lose its rider on the third fence.

The video craze, like all crazes, had died; the bandit was too old to sell. The kids had grown up into the pubs and his eating and drinking customers had not returned. He waited for Lapino while watching his money fall at every fence.

'What did the owner say to you then?' asked Louise as Lewis sat down with the coffees and two cakes which he had also bought.

'Oh, he just recognised me from when I was in here as a kid. I used to play the machines a lot.'

'My mother used to warn me never to come into this place.'

'She was probably right. People like me were in here.'

'Perhaps I should have come in then.'

Louise had relaxed and reverted to the teasing mood that had frustrated Lewis on Wednesday night. He was not sure if he was up to her games; she appeared a bit sharp. But he could not resist the flirtation.

'So where are you going on Saturday then?' asked Lewis.

'I told you, Swansea. It's a friend's leaving do.'

'Going anywhere particular?'

'Juliet's probably. We'll see what we feel like when we're down there, I expect.'

'Why's your friend leaving, then?'

'She's just got married and her husband's found a job in Swindon. She's not looking forward to it really, but he can't get work anywhere down here.'

'It'll be alright, I expect; Swindon's a change at least,' commiserated Lewis as if he had known the girl in question a lifetime. Moving to Swindon seemed an unlikely way out.

'Where is Swindon anyway?'

'Past Bristol, I think; I'm not sure. She doesn't really want to move away from her family, but she's got a transfer, so at least she won't lose her job.'

'Oh, there you are there then, no problem,' affirmed Lewis with sweeping authority.

'Do I know her?' asked Lewis, feeling that he was getting there. ˙

'No.'

'Well enjoy yourself.'

'I will,' she paused briefly before adding 'What are you doing on Saturday then?'

'Funny you should mention that. I'm going to Swansea as well, on a stag-night. I might see you there.'

'Yes, you might,' replied Louise with no encouragement.

Lewis was stumbling for topics now. He thought about enquiring why she was out on a Friday afternoon but he had asked that already. There was no easy rapport. In desperation he took a gulp from his coffee, smiling as he replaced the cup before looking away into the depths of the café. The red vinyl chairs and chequered table tops offered no inspiration.

'Have you seen Marianne lately?' Lewis would have dropped his cup if he had been holding it. He was not prepared for such a direct question. But he answered.

'No, she's moved away as well.'

'I thought she was in college.'

'Yes she is, but she's hardly ever home, and when she is I don't see her. Anyway, how do you know about me and Marianne?'

'I know quite a bit about you, Lewis.'

'Do you?' replied Lewis, surprised but flattered.

'Yes, I remember you and Marianne kissing so openly in the school yard.'

Lewis could remember this as well, but now he didn't really want to be reminded of it. The memories were too close. He searched for a way out.

'I was a year below you, I doubt if you can remember me.'

'Of course I can.' Lewis lied. 'What else do you know about me then?' Lewis was intrigued by another person's viewpoint of him.

'I can remember you getting expelled.'

'I was never expelled, only suspended,' Lewis bristled. Did he really want to discuss this with Louise? He had hoped for some gentle flirtation to remove his mind from the futility of a fading Friday afternoon. This conversation was too real.

'But you never came back after Easter.'

'That was my choice, not theirs. I worked instead.'

'Marianne stayed on though, didn't she?'

'Yes, she stayed on, that's why she's in college now.'

'Why did you leave then?'

'I'd just had enough, that's all. Most people leave school at sixteen anyway.'

'There were all sorts of rumours flying around school. You were supposed to have hit Mr. Marshall.'

Lewis paused before answering. 'Just rumours, that's all. I was glad to get out of the place. I probably would have got expelled if I'd stayed any longer.'

'You and Marianne stayed together though, didn't you?'

'Aye, off an' on. We messed about for a bit longer, prolonging the agony.'

Louise sensed that Lewis didn't want to answer any more questions on Marianne. There was a reticence in his voice that suggested it was a closed area that he rarely discussed with himself. Despite his crudeness, Louise liked Lewis. More than Lewis would ever realise. She didn't enjoy his games but she played them anyway. She reluctantly allowed him his escape.

He stirred his lukewarm coffee. The circular motion of the minute bubbles disrupted the skin that had formed on the surface of the chocolate-coloured drink. Louise looked up as the café door opened, allowing in a rare customer. The man was middle-aged with a spread middle; he bought a packet of cigarettes and left. Lewis finished the remains of his coffee. Louise realised it was time to leave before the silence debilitated future meetings.

'Shall we go then?'

'Yes, okay, you're sure you don't want another coffee?

'No, thank you, I've got to catch the ten past bus.'

'Can I walk you to the bus stop?'

'If you don't mind.'

They abandoned the café to Morrezzi and his customer. It was a short walk to the bus stop, up Alstair Street to the gardens. The evening had closed around them as Lewis refurled the umbrella. He handed it to Louise who kissed him gently on the cheek before boarding the bus. She turned to wave goodbye but Lewis had already gone and was walking back down Alstair Street, across the square, past the Cherub, over the old town bridge and up the twisting hill home.

Lewis's father was reading the evening paper when he arrived home. He peered over the top to confirm his suspicion that it was Lewis. A faint smell of food suggested that the microwave was determinedly removing the last vestiges of taste from a previously prepared meal. The table had been cleared except for a half-full cup of tea which cooled quickly, forgotten by his father. His mother was not in the kitchen but her presence was obvious as his father could not operate the microwave.

'Finish early today, Lew?' enquired his father.

'Aye, about three, job an'finish.'

The discourse ended. Lewis sat down and removed his dirt-smattered trainers. He gazed idly at the microwave, considering what it was likely to be. Not lasagne again.

'Hello, love. Finish early today, did you?'

Lewis turned towards his mother who had returned to the kitchen.

'Yes, Mam.'

'Where've you been then?'

'Only to town.'

'Buy anything?'

'No.'

'See anybody you know?'

'Not really, no.'

'Going out tonight, love?'

'I'm not sure yet, Mam. Later on perhaps.'

'Oh there you are then. Well here's your tea, do you want something to drink?'

'Yes please mam,' he paused before reminding his mother that he had put her money on the dressing table.

'Yes, thanks love. I've picked it up.'

Lewis ate in silence and on his own. His parents had obviously eaten before he arrived home. He stared at a wall of newspaper which occasionally rustled as his father turned over the pages. His mother had retreated into the living room to watch her nightly soap installment. Occasional snatches of second-hand drama forced their way into his thoughts. He resented the intrusion. He didn't even watch the series and he knew the names of some of the characters. The meal was a tasteless ordeal: it wasn't lasagne but it could have been. He scraped the leftovers into the pedal bin and slipped the stained plate into the bowl of dishwater and fading soap suds. He briefly considered washing the dishes but dismissed the idea in the knowledge that his mother would do them later. His father had progressed to the front page of the newspaper as Lewis vacated the unspoken kitchen and retreated to his room.

The room possessed a quiet dormant expectancy of something well worn and used but now nearly finished, disregarded, but waiting patiently for someone to take an interest in it again. A single bed absorbed most of the space, pushed up against a wooden wardrobe. The covers were pulled tight, awaiting re-entry. A window overlooked the back garden; the curtains were half-open, half-closed; it was difficult to say. A cluster of tattered paperbacks used the wide windowsill as a bookcase; they were swollen where condensation from the window had settled on them. The walls were covered with posters: a sun-bleached elephant on the African savannah; a tumble of fox cubs staring expectantly out of a den; a maritime chart of the British Isles, courtesy of the Seaman's Mission; a rugby team resplendent in red jerseys. They were all secured by yellowing sellotape, an occasional space with stains forming a square marked where a poster had fallen and not been replaced.

A bookcase stood obstinately opposite his bed, providing a stand for his black and white television. The bottom shelves were filled with magazines lying flat on top of each other, spilling over onto the floor. Copies of *Angling Today* and *Rugby World* mixed uneasily with each other in a formless pile. The top shelves contained an eclectic mixture: birdwatching books, Penguins and an incomplete set of hardback Dickens novels, bold in red leather bindings and gold-embossed letters. Lewis sometimes stared at the names on the covers: *Nicholas Nickleby*, *Little Dorrit*, *Great Expectations*, but he had never read any of them. A present from a long-dead aunt, they provided a warm comfort in their presence and apparent immortality. He had read most of the paperbacks, but recently he had not required anything of books. Their predictability bored him.

He turned on the tv which balanced precariously on the top shelf of the bookcase: competing for space with a ceramic rugby ball in which he collected his spare coppers and a framed picture of himself in the schools under fifteen rugby team. He looked at the picture. What were the faces doing now? He still came into contact with a few. Some were married, some he knew had moved away. Daz was there but most had passed into the thickening shadows of his youth.

He switched the main light off, allowing the tv to illuminate the room. The posters, the tattered books and the fading photographs receded gratefully into the darkness. This was the room of his youth, of his mind's imagination, a youth he had only recently left, of which he wanted no part or all of it. He didn't want the memories of his room but he couldn't find the time to throw them away; there was no point. The room absorbed little of his waking hours now. It was only the occasional lonely Friday evening, when drinking or training didn't offer an escape, that he was drawn into it.

He tried to concentrate on the black and white images which danced across the flickering screen. But the Friday night's offerings were too shallow even for mindless viewing. Lewis tried another channel. A quiz show appeared; the contestants were answering and giggling inanely. He lay back on the bed, staring at the screen. A girl appeared; he recognised her. She began asking the questions. He was the contestant; he blurted out answers. Yes, he had left school. Of course it was his choice. But why hadn't she supported him? Remember who's asking the questions; who is the contestant. Why had he given in? He was protecting her. She could look after herself. It wasn't her fault, was it? What else was there to do? It wasn't her fault. You made your own decisions, marked your own time.

Lewis awoke to the sound of a police siren in a car chase. The quiz show had been replaced by an American cop serial. Lewis was sure he'd seen it before, if not the actual episode at least the same plot. He focused hazily on his alarm clock which illuminated the time as nine-thirty. He was not sure he wanted to go out, but fuck it what else was there to do?

He forced himself off the bed, his clothes were stiff and uncomfortable from sleeping in them. He was hot; his jeans tight around his thighs compressed his balls and squashed his dick against the rough denim. It was difficult to rise out of the lethargy. He checked himself in the shaving mirror: rough as hell; hair tousled and matted; eyes red rimmed and half-open. As he pulled his T-shirt over his head there was a faint smell of tired sweat but he dismissed the idea of a shower; there was not enough time. To smother the sweat he doused himself with a spray and forced the last drops out of a Paco Rabanne bottle. There was a clean shirt in the wardrobe which provided a welcome cold freshness as he buttoned it around him. He ran his fingers through his hair several times until he found an acceptable level of dishevelment. He was ready to go out.

He descended the stairs into the silence of the house. A faint hum emanated from the living room, which suggested one of his parents was being entertained by the soporific Friday night tv. It had been successful with Lewis. It was probably his mother abandoned to her solitary comforts while his father skulked off to the club to talk nothing with some equally bored part-time bachelors. He decided not to disturb her. There was no point; he had nothing to say. Picking his coat out from under the stairs he let himself out of the back door. A faint feeling of guilt absorbed him as he turned the key on his mother and her Friday night companion.

A line of people waited impatiently at the door of the Divine Cherub. Even though it was Friday night and town was thronged with people attempting to expunge another dreary week, the Cherub was not as popular as Archways and there was rarely a long queue. Lewis knew the bouncer if there was. He walked along Bridge Street; the lights and music of the Cherub fixing his attention. Hopefully there would be someone he knew, someone to spend a few minutes of Friday night with.

By the time he reached the door the queue had been absorbed, leaving him standing alone. He waited for the door to re-open and allow him into the sanctuary of the pub. A sign creaked in the wind above him, its painted picture depicting an angelic character with rosy cheeks and a halo above his head. He had fat arms and legs, played a harp and was only wearing a fig leaf. His eyes of innocence obviously knew nothing of the happenings which occurred nightly in his cherished abode.

The door opened.

'Two only, boys.' Lewis looked behind him. There was no one there. Obviously the man was tuned into his work.

'Cheers, Dai.'

'No problem, Lew.'

Lewis knew the bouncer from the rugby field. He had played against him a few times for Malci, but he may have recently moved to the Ferry.

His eyes adjusted rapidly to the light in the pub. The noise and the faces briefly engulfed him before he reached the protection of the bar. As Lewis settled into the wait for a drink he scanned the pub in the hope of finding someone he could start a conversation with, someone he wouldn't have to try too hard with. The pub was packed. He vaguely recognised a few faces, a smattering of the older people mostly in couples. But most of the faces were youngsters and way under age. He was getting too old for this place. There was no one he really knew well enough to speak to for anything more than a minute. What would they have in common?

A tall man in a denim jacket squeezed in next to him. It was a face he had stared at already tonight, but the face had been younger then and holding the ball in an under fifteen's team photograph. He was sure he would recognise him if he said hello. But he was unsure if he wanted to speak to him. What would they have to say to each other? He had spoken to him three, maybe four times since they had left school and they had never been anywhere near good friends then. But if he didn't make an approach now that would be it. They would probably never speak to each other again, even though they would both remember, and remember the time they did not bother to speak any more.

'Hello, Mart. How's it going?'

The man turned around to face Lewis.

'Oh hello, Lew, didn't see you there. I'm alright, how's yourself?'

'Oh, I'm fine.'

The man ordered his pint as the barmaid passed. There was an awkward pause as they both thought of something more to say.

'What you doing with yourself these days, Mart?'

Lewis had asked him this question on every one of their last meetings and he presumed Mart had given him the same answer every time. But he had no idea what it was.

'Still at Partridges, but I've moved onto the electrical section.'

'Oh aye, any good?'

'Well the pay's more or less the same, but it's a bit more interesting.'

Mart didn't offer anything further so Lewis struggled on while Mart paid for his lager and half a cider.

'Still playing rugby?'

'No, not any more. I don't seem to have the time with the house.'

'Bought a house, have you?' asked Lewis, unable to conceal his surprise.

'Aye, me and the Mrs, last summer, up at Glendale.'

'I didn't know you were married,' Lewis asked incredulously.

'Yes, almost a year now and I've a baby on the way.'

Mart asserted the last piece of information as if he conceded his wife a small supporting role in the forthcoming birth.

'Anyway, I've got to get back to the Mrs, see you, Lewis.'

Mart turned and headed off through the crowd, resplendent with two drinks and buoyed by undoubted confidence in his own virility.

Lewis was stunned by Mart's revelations in a one-way conversation. He gratefully returned his attention to the procurement of a drink. He did not want to consider the divergence in their prospective lives. He was going to get left on the shelf at twenty-one.

He was not in a rush to receive a drink as this would involve giving up the protection of the bar. He would have to stand alone, isolated and obscenely obvious that he was on his own. A circle would form around him, a zone of exclusion. At least while he stood at the bar he could maintain the pretence that he was getting a round in. No, he was not alone in a pub on a Friday night looking for someone to talk to. Of course he wasn't. His pint appeared and he thought, fuck them, I don't mind being alone.

'Hello, Lew.' Lewis turned around to meet Mike.

'Hi'ah, Mike, didn't see you there, you been in long?'

'No, I've just come in. Don't usually come out much on a Friday night but my girlfriend's out with her friends.'

It was not like Mike to be out at all any more, especially without his girlfriend. The Friday television must have been boring. Lewis was amazed to see him out alone. Perhaps he didn't care about standing in a pub on his own.

'You with anybody, Mike?'

'No, just popped out for a pint. I got pissed off with the telly.'

'Aye, and me. It's bloody crowded here, though.'

'Aye, it's all these kids. There's a girl over there who's a friend of my sister and she's only fourteen. Tell you what, Lew, let's get out of the traffic a bit. I'm getting soaked here.'

They moved over to lean against a pillar which acted as a baffle to the constant flow of people on a route to the toilet.

'Looking forward to tomorrow night, Mike?'

'Aye, it should be a laugh, as long as I don't get too pissed.'

'What would we want to do that for, Mike?'

'Aye, I know. I've been on a few of these stag-nights before, mind. Remember Scott Baker? The police found him at four in the morning wandering around the Gardens, stark naked with a ball and chain around his ankle. Couldn't even speak. His prospective father-in-law had to bail him out in the morning so he could attend the wedding.'

Lewis laughed at the memory. He had also been on that stag-night when he was still in youth. What a state Scott had got into. It all proved to be a waste of time in the end. He was divorced within a year.

'I don't think it will come to that, Mike. Anyway, your wedding isn't until a week, Saturday is it?'

'Aye that's right. I had no intention of stumbling down the aisle with a stinking hangover and looking as rough as a badger's arse.'

'You' girlfriend know about the stag-night?'

'Yes, but she's not happy. That's where she is tonight, out on her hen-night with the girls from the office.'

'Where's she gone?'

'Juliet's, I think; she wouldn't tell me.'

'It's like that, is it?'

'At the moment, yes; I wouldn't be surprised if she turns up tomorrow to keep an eye on me.'

'She wouldn't do that, would she?'

Mike didn't answer, just peered into his pint before taking a drink. Lewis was intrigued by this unexpected insight into Mike's prospective marital arrangements. To him they had appeared a contented couple, sitting in tandem, usually alone at a table, rarely talking but ostensibly happy. Mike with his pint of lager, her with a Martini and lemonade. But looking at it now it appeared a shallow pool. It was a standard joke that Mike was under the proverbial thumb but it now looked more like a constant battle in which there had been a temporary truce called to promote a calm public facade. Daz's pronouncements on marriage returned to his mind.

'Where're you going to be living then, Mike?'

'We're saving for a deposit at the moment, Lew. After the wedding we've got a room in her parents' house. It'll be alright for a while, I suppose,' asserted Mike, trying desperately to convince himself.

Lewis thought that perhaps the money for the wedding could have been used for a house deposit but decided it was not prudent to suggest it. It was a bit late to change the arrangements now.

'The wedding must be setting you back a bit, though. The reception's at the Manor, isn't it?'

The Manor was the top wedding venue in the area. It stood on a hill judiciously surveying the town. Its Georgian splendour lamenting a time that had gone, of garden parties and house staff that had receded with the years, its dignity now disintegrating in the face of vulgar conference guests who hacked their way around the nine-hole golf course. It had effectively monopolised the town's wedding market. The food was nothing removed from the basic beef and two veg, while the function room was a converted barn with high draughty ceilings and white-washed walls. But the grounds, with the sculptured hedges, copper beeches and ornamental fountains looked great in the wedding photographs.

'It's not costing me much; her old man is paying. I suggested somewhere a bit less expensive but Melissa wouldn't consider it. She said she was only getting married once and it might as well be special.'

Mike smiled at Lewis over the top of his glass before he upended and finished it. Mike was guessing what Lewis was thinking. He was pretty close.

'Want another pint, Lew?'

'Yes, please, Mike. I'll have a bitter.'

Lewis looked around the bar. A mass of people all out on a Friday night trying to forget the week, attempting to find some enjoyment. The faces he recognised were younger than him. When was he going to opt out of this ride? Take a marriage ticket out of drunken weekends and rushed romances.

''Ere you are, Lew.'

'Thanks, Mike.'

They both automatically took a drink.

'Many going to the wedding, Mike?' asked Lewis. The arrangements for the wedding held a compulsive fascination for him. He presumed it was an occasion he would at some time be more than an interested spectator.

'Half the bloody valley, I think, Lew. I didn't realise how many relatives she had until we had the invitations printed. I don't think she's seen most of them since the christening but they're still coming. You're coming on the night, aren't you, Lew?'

'Aye, I'll be there,' confirmed Lewis enthusiastically.

'We haven't given out the night invitation cards yet, Lew. I was thinking of just putting a general invitation up the club?'

'Don't worry about it, Mike. I think everyone's going anyway. What about the honeymoon, you going anywhere special?'

'Tenerife,' Mike answered with such an air of finality that Lewis did not need to guess who had made that choice. Mike looked despondently into the depths of his pint. Lewis took another swig of his lager.

'What about you, Lew? When are you going to get married?'

'Plenty of time for that, Mike. I think I'll probably wait until I'm as old and grey as you are.'

Mike looked straight at Lewis without even a smile before taking another drink. Lewis did not think he was annoyed. He was unsure if Mike had even heard him but he allowed the subject to drop. They both drank occasionally while surveying the bar. The music from the juke-box competed with shouted conversations, forming a squabble of voices and snatched lyrics. Lewis tried not to look at Mike; he sensed the tension as Mike wrestled with his thoughts. In a strange way he envied his imminent stability but he also abhorred it.

'Lew, don't look now but there's a guy over by the door staring at us. He either knows you or he's desperate for a fight because I've never seen him before in my life.'

Lewis gradually turned around to afford himself a view of the guy at the door. He didn't know him but he recognised Marianne immediately even though she faced away from him. Long chestnut fronds of hair caressed the deep blue of her dress. One shoulder was bare, pale skin reflecting the pale light. She still curved at the hips although he sensed that she had put on some weight. Perhaps she was on the pill now. The dress stretched over her thighs stopping an inch above the back of her knees. Her legs were covered in what he assumed were stockings. Despite the uneasy panic of seeing her again he had an instant hard-on.

'Do you know him?'

'Yes, I used to go out with her once.'

'Out with her. No wonder he's looking at you; she looks gorgeous from the back.'

'She's even better from the front.'

'Why's he staring, then? You owe him any favours?'

'No, I don't think so, as I've never seen him before either. I think he must be her boyfriend from college.'

'Oh, that's the girl you were knocking around with for years, is it?'

'Aye, that's her. Anyway, better not stare otherwise that guy's going to be steaming over 'ere by the looks of it.'

'Yep, he's a big bastard, but don't you worry, I'll hold your pint if he comes over.'

Lewis continued drinking his pint but his eyes were drawn to Marianne. Her shape recalled too many memories to ignore, too many half-forgotten, half-remembered warm, stolen afternoons. He was again captivated; the pain of not being able to go over and talk to her when there was so much to say. So many apologies to make, so many recriminations to endure. The need to go over and talk to her was immense. He needed to say something, not just walk past and acknowledge her as if she was someone he half-knew once, a long time ago. Her head flickered around but she sensed he was looking and she returned to face her man who was staring aggressively across at Lewis. This was someone who had shared his deepest thoughts, his most concealed ambitions, the simplest fears. They had loved each other then: half-oranges together. Someone who was now dislocated from him: in another world never again to share the sun glinting off the evening surf in summer. To listen to the descent of water in dripping limestone caves. No one to push into the drifts of his grandfather's farm. No buzzards flying through sun-dappled oakwood as they lay naked in the grass. She was not in his time any more.

'I'm going to say hello.'

'What? The guy looks mad as hell, Lew. He'll go lite,' predicted Mike incredulously.

'It's not him I'm going to say hello to, is it?'

'He doesn't look the discriminating type to me, Lew. I bet he punches you as soon as you open your mouth.'

'No, he'll be alright, but if he does, sort him out for me.'

'Wait a minute, Lew, I'll come over with you.'

But Lewis was already making his way across the bar so Mike allowed him to go.

As Lewis approached, Marianne turned, her eyes pleading with Lewis not to come closer, but his mind was locked now.

'Hello, Mari. How are you? I haven't seen you for ages. How's it going in London?' Lewis attempted to sound as casual as possible.

Marianne stared harshly at him before answering briefly. 'I think you'd better go, Lewis.'

Lewis looked at her in disbelief.

'It's as bad as that is it?' he mumbled.

'Yeh, why don't you fuck off. She doesn't want to talk to you,' added her boyfriend.

Lewis tried to go but who the hell was this telling him to fuck off? He stared at the man; he was probably the same age as Lewis, taller by two inches but not as heavy. He had privilege oozing out of him, corrupted into his very sinews. University wasn't an achievement for him, it was the natural progression. He held a cigarette arrogantly between two fingers.

Lewis could tell from his stance that he was drunk; despite his education he slurred his words.

'What the 'ell as it got to do with you pal?' retorted Lewis, turning his attention to the person who at that instant he truly hated. The hate accelerated through his body. Go on, mate, say something.

'It's got everything to do with me if you must know. Mari's told me all about you and if you don't fuck off like a good little boy I'm go...'

Lewis hit him hard across the side of his leering face. The moment his fist connected with skin and bone he regretted it. His target stumbled backwards with the force of the blow but stayed unsteadily on his feet.

Marianne screamed desperately and rushed at Lewis. He held her briefly before throwing her to his side as her boyfriend rushed at him. Lewis stepped easily out of the reach of his drunken lunge, grabbing him from behind and pushing him over one of the small tables scattering drinks and ashtrays into the laps of the sitting couples.

He felt a sharp bursting sensation across the side of his eye and he realised that this was not going to be a private fight. It was a Friday night. He turned around only to be hit sideways against the bar by a glancing blow from a man with a short-hair-cut and a denim jacket. The man moved towards Lewis again, fists raised, shouting, but stalled as Mike connected with an unseen blow from his right. The man collapsed into a dazed heap on the floor, uncertain where he was, unsure whether Friday night was such a good idea.

'Let's get the fuck out of here, Lew. All hell's broken loose.'

'Where's Marianne?'

'It's okay, she got pushed out of the door by the bouncers.'

Mayhem engulfed the pub. Three separate fights and an idiot wielding a chair. Lewis's original adversary had struggled to his feet only to be hit back down again and was now covering his head from a succession of kicks administered by a frenzied attacker. Lewis ran across, catching the man with a blow on the temple. He crumpled immediately.

'Look, pal, get up. You've got to get out of here.'

Lewis heaved Marianne's boyfriend to his feet. There was blood streaming from his nose and he had a split lip. Lewis could see he didn't recognise him; his eyes were too blurred.

'Lewis, come on, police.'

Mike shouted above the threats and the Michael Jackson record which played unaware of the alternative entertainment. This was a good night out for some people.

Lewis instinctively looked at the door where a policeman was attempting to force a way through the panicked crowd blocking the entrance. Mike was already running through the pub towards the fire exit. Lewis ran after him through the frightened faces, smashed glasses and screaming girls. It was too packed to run but Lewis wasn't worrying about tipping any beer now; he had to get out. Out and away from the consequences. Mike had opened the fire escape as Lewis reached it. A bouncer in a dark suit attempted to grab him as he raced through. He shrugged him off effortlessly. The adrenalin had seared his muscles, rapid as a grass fire in summer.

He was out into a randomly lit car-park. He hesitated for an instant, unsure which way to run. The darkness of one corner attracted him. If he could vault the wall into the castle grounds he would be clear. Voices clamoured after him, exhorting him to stop, come back. A car screeched to a halt among flailing sirens at the entrance to the car-park. Lewis could sense that the occupants had emerged and were running. He had no time to guess their position; the only thing to concern him was the far wall. He was sprinting hard. His jeans restricted him but his trainers afforded a secure grip on the wet tarmac. The voices to his side were getting near but the wall was closing. The hard scuffle of the shoes hitting the floor threatened him. The angle would have sealed it with a drunk but Lewis was flying. He jumped for the wall with nine-feet to go. The first contact found him clawing at the top, ivy obscuring his vision; the second he was falling through space as he plunged the deep side into the castle grounds. It was a ten-foot drop the other side of the wall. He hit the floor hard and rolled forwards sprawling on the wet grass. With the fall he lost his orientation, his face against the turf, chest down, winded. The voices on the other side of the wall, desperately scrambling up the loose ivy, forced him to his feet. Running. The grounds were a dark maze of trees and shadows. A low wall sent him sprawling again; he felt pain flash through his hand as he hit the floor. In the darkness he guessed it was a cut; the slime of his own blood confirmed it. He was clear now if he could make the river bank. A footpath followed the line of the river skirting the castle. It led up the valley towards Nant. From there it was only a short walk home. They wouldn't chase him far; it was only a pub fight.

As he sprinted through the manicured gardens a line of iron railings rose sharply out of the blackness. His hand fired in pain as he caught the hard wrought iron. He gripped the spiked ends, and vaulted them in two movements. Judging the drop, he landed firmly on the path then continued running. Up the valley towards Nant. Not a sprint now; he knew he was clear. The police would have only just cleared the wall, then they would search the castle grounds. No chance.

But he still ran, an even pace, away from the Divine Cherub.

After running for several minutes he slowed to a slow jog and as the path degenerated into mud patches and puddles he walked. The river was to his left, just visible in the darkness between the bare trees and hawthorn bushes which lined the embankment. An occasional rush of noise marked a fast flowing stretch of water as it descended the valley in brief reminiscent enthusiasm for its time in the hills. On his right the line of the path had been joined by a narrow canal. The path clung to a narrow isthmus as it slowly climbed the valley.

As the adrenalin became absorbed he became aware again of the reason for running. Why had he hit her boyfriend? It was too obviously the thing to do. The action returned in pieces: the hard punch; his hand screaming in pain as he connected; Marianne throwing herself at him. He wouldn't have hit him again: there was no time anyway as the place erupted. Why was there that much anger? It must have been a bad week. His hopes of speaking to Marianne, to explain the mistaken assumptions, seemed to have disappeared into the confusion of a pub fight. It didn't seem a fitting end.

A branch overhanging the path scratched across his face. As he fended it off, pain shot through his hand. He tried to examine it again: blood smeared with dirt and grass, drying black and red, but through the darkness he could make out a slashed cut which was still forcing out droplets of untainted blood. It would be swollen in the morning. He tried not to think about it. Instead the sound of the police running and calling for him as if he was about to stop and give himself up forced a smile. They had tried to scramble over the wall but had been frustrated by the ivy; it would have been a tricky climb in the light. Lewis had known he had to make the top at the first attempt or they would have caught him. It was a one chance leap. Mike? Where the hell was Mike? It was only now he thought about Mike; he had been too occupied with getting away. There had been several figures running across the car-park, vaguely running on the edges of his vision, unsure if they were chasing him or running away. He stifled a smile as he remembered Baker and the thought of Mike's father-in-law picking him up from the nick in the morning. Mike would have got away; he was too sharp.

As Lewis rounded a bend on the river bank a set of white street lamps sewn across a road bridge marked the beginning of Nant. He gratefully accepted the firm hardness of a pavement again. The route home was signposted by a trail of lights stretching along the far side of the valley back down towards town.

Walking home through the early hours of another day the streets had become barren. Moving cars were rare; a black and white taxi ghosting up the valley provided the only traffic. Nothing else; everything dormant. The houses were dark, closed down for the night. The whole valley slept unaware of anything: oblivious to drunks, feuding couples, foxes, police cars. Oblivious to the late-night early-morning sodium silence which entombed the valley.

A hum in the distance heralded a car moving along the valley road. Lewis picked up the headlights as it twisted around a bend. He was hoping it was not a police car but it was. He did not run as the chances of it recognising him were small. If he ran now they would definitely chase him. The car slowed as it passed him, the passenger appraising with a suspicious eye. It didn't stop. Lewis immediately ducked up an alley. It was only a few more streets before the sanctuary of a warm bed. The craving for a bed on a long walk home became obsessive, the need to rest consuming, but to stop would merely prolong the walk. Now he needed to allow the bed to absorb him. He was tired from the run and his hand stung with blood and dirt. The adrenalin had been absorbed and the cooling sweat on his shirt made him shiver. Marianne's look of hate fed upon his thoughts.

His house was silent and as dark as all the others he had passed. He found the key under a loose brick on the back wall. The dry warmth of the central heating welcomed him into the kitchen. He was vaguely aware that he would soon be asleep and his thoughts would no longer dissect him.

Marianne would disappear into his driven, never-remembered dreams. She still haunted his every waking hour but to his sleep she was gratefully unrecalled.

SATURDAY

Lewis was awake. He had gradually allowed the opaque light of the morning to trickle through the cracks and splinters in the venetian blinds until it had forced him awake. His first thought had recoiled from the need to get up for work before he realised it was Saturday. Relief was instantly swallowed by the panic in the memory of the night before. It engulfed him in a mire of empty action. He had been too sober even to forget the minor details. He only had to lie in bed and think about it. He was awake with plenty of time to think before he had to get up. Every other day of the week he awoke late and had to force himself out of bed to work. Saturday morning he awoke the time he should have been getting up all week and had nothing to do but kill the minutes until he was so bored he had to get up.

The faint rush of speeding cars in the rain fringed the edges of his mind as he picked over the night. A dull pain in his hand recalled the fall in the castle grounds; he did not want to remember any of it but what was there to do?

'Lewis, love, you awake?'

He considered the question. Answering it would probably mean he had to get up for something. But what for?

'Lewis.'

'Yes, Mam, what do you want?'

'Mr. Watkins is downstairs, love. He wants you to work this morning.'

Lewis swore inaudibly to himself.

'Well, what shall I tell him?'

Lewis still refused to reply.

'Lewis?'

'Tell him I'll be down now.'

Lewis listened to his mother descend the stairs before a swell of voices rose from the kitchen. His mother would be fussing over Roy. "Fancy a cup of tea, Mr. Watkins? What about a couple of rounds of toast?" His mother liked Roy; she had been pleased when Lewis had found a job with him despite her hopes of the sixth form. Roy would be five years older than his mother, maybe six. Perhaps she had known him in her courting days. Six years was not an improbable difference and Roy had married late. There was something in her references to him.

Lewis abandoned his idle musings when he realised what Roy was doing in his kitchen on a Saturday morning. He had to get up to work, on a Saturday morning. What the hell was Roy playing at? He disliked working on Saturday mornings as much as Lewis did.

Lewis reluctantly removed the bedclothes, forced himself into a sitting position before drowsily stumbling over to the half-open wardrobe. He pulled out a pair of battered jeans which had been hung, washed and ironed awaiting Monday morning. His mother ran the house on a conveyor belt system: leave anything lying around that had been worn and it would immediately be taken up by the conveyor-belt before magically reappearing in his cupboard. He would not have been surprised to find his father hanging there one morning. He got all this for thirty pound a week housekeeping money. He didn't consider this generous; he didn't consider it at all, save for one isolated outbreak of egalitarianism when he had proposed a rota system where in conjunction with his father they would get up two mornings a week to do the washing. He had tried it twice; his father had not bothered at all. His mother accepted it all without comment.

'Lewis, Mr. Watkins is waiting.'

The shout from the kitchen roused Lewis from his idling. He didn't want to go down at all but what else was there to do?

As Lewis entered the kitchen Roy was sitting at the table draining the last drops of a cup of tea served in his mother's best china. An empty plate flecked with crumbs and jam confirmed Lewis's prediction of Roy's breakfast. His mother sat opposite him and they both looked up, disturbed by Lewis's obviously premature appearance.

Roy placed his cup delicately on the china saucer.

'That was a lovely cup of tea, Mair.'

'It's a pleasure, Royston. Few people enjoy tea these days; they just drink it.'

Lewis was surprised to hear his mother use Roy's full first name.

'Right then, Lew, you ready? Sorry about the Saturday morning bit but my brother is desperate for an extra hand. There's twenty quid in it for you and it should only take a couple of hours.'

'Well I haven't had any breakfast yet, Roy.'

'Oh, don't worry about that, mun. A big breakfast will slow you down.'

'I've done a couple of slices of toast for you, love. You can eat them in the van. I think Mr. Watkins is in a bit of a rush.'

'Thanks, Mam,' replied Lewis without any conviction as his mother handed him two limp pieces of cold toast. He fumbled for his boots under one of the chairs.

'I brought your boots in for you as well.'

Lewis looked up and stared at his mother who smiled at him innocently and then aimed a 'Love him, he's a lovely boy,' look at Roy. Lewis looked at Roy who beamed a 'Better do as your mother asks,' smile back. Lewis surrendered to his boots.

He was sitting in the van, hunched up with his denim jacket curled around him, finishing his last slice of toast before he spoke again. 'What's your brother want us for then?'

Roy changed gear before answering. 'He's building a wall on his bloody estate and there's some good stone going in town where they're knocking down the hall of the old grammar school. He needs the van really but it's quicker for him if we come with it.'

'The one by the park?'

'That's the one. Didn't you go there, Lew?'

'Yes, I was there for a couple of years; the first two of comprehensive. Bloody hated the place. Didn't you go there then, Roy?'

'Don't be daft, mun, Lew, it really was the grammar school in my day. You had to have money to go there then as well as pass the bloody eleven plus.'

'Didn't you pass that then, Roy?' Lewis was genuinely surprised.

'Aye, fat chance of that. I could only speak Welsh until I was eight then I had to sit the eleven plus two years later. I couldn't even speak it properly. Some would say I still can't, but not to my face, ay, Lew?' Lewis laughed. 'No, I was packed off to the secondary modern up the valley, and I can tell you something modern it wasn't. The teachers were the ones who couldn't get in the grammar either; half of them were three quarters the way to a nervous breakdown.'

'Nothing's changed then, Roy. My music teacher used to sellotape three rulers together so he could hit people harder. They made him head of department in the end, before they locked him away.'

'There's few sane teachers around, Lew. Mind you, a job like that would drive you to madness or at least drink.'

The van rumbled through the sparse Saturday morning traffic. It was too early for the shopping frenzy.

'Your brother's meeting us there, is he, Roy?'

'So he said, Lew. He'd better be as I'm not moving eight ton of cut stone on a Saturday morning if he hasn't got up to help us.'

As they reached the park Roy turned off the main road into the generous school grounds. An exquisitely white sherpa van stood marooned in the school yard, obviously waiting for some instructions. A sign on the side informed them and the world that its owner was none other than William Watkins Painter and Decorator. There was even a phone number on which to contact him.

'Well he's here, Roy, and he's brought his mobile hoarding with him.'

'He never was shy, Will, and he always seems to have a new van. There must be more money in painting than building.'

Roy considered his statement before adding. 'But he hasn't made a bloody start, has he?'

Roy pulled the van alongside his brother's. Lewis and Roy got out to be greeted by a smiling William Watkins.

'What are you waiting for then, Will? Do you need instructions on how to pick stones up?'

'Good morning, Royston, pleased to see you. Actually we're waiting for the van. We need something to load the stones onto, you see.'

'You could have begun sorting them.'

'Oh give over, we've only just arrived.'

Royston smiled grimly. Lewis hung in the background, waiting for the brothers to overcome their awkward friendly greeting. There was a strong love between them. It existed as an obvious and clumsy bond that they would try to ignore but would invariably entangle themselves within. Lewis would not have been able to describe it but it was there. Being an only child there was no love in him for another sibling but the appearance of it fascinated him.

'How are you, Lew?'

'Fine thanks, Will. You got much work on?'

'It's ticking over, Lew. The private work's pretty slow, but we've got a couple of council contracts which are keeping the lads working.'

'You still up at Rhigos?'

'No, we finished there a fortnight ago. How's the rugby, Lew? Big game this afternoon, isn't there?'

'Aye, win or relegation, Will.'

'I think I'll come up and watch this afternoon. Who's in the back row with you?'

'Hazel and John Harris.'

'Mike Thomas playing?'

'Yes, Mike's playing. He's been playing well the last couple of weeks.'

'Ay, are you two going to get started or shall we clock on for tomorrow as well? And Andrew, you just take notes; this one's too tough for you.'

The second occupant of Will's van now ambled around to join the threesome. He beamed confident smiles at everyone.

'He's getting educated now, Royston. Soon he'll be telling us what to do.'

''Ow's it going, Roy,' enquired Andrew with a casual friendly arrogance.

'Fine. How's college treating you, son?'

'Not too bad, Roy; there's plenty going on.'

'Not working you too hard, are they?'

'Up late every night, Roy, in the bar at least. It's the experience, see,' replied Andrew, grinning at his father.

'Well, you can experience some real work this morning, my boy. No more lounging around in pubs on a Saturday morning when you're home here.' Will made this prediction with the air of a man who had yet to be convinced of the benefits of higher education. His son may be getting an easy time of it in college but when he was home he was going to damn well work.

He was paying a substantial sum towards Andrew's grant and he was looking for value for money through any means possible. The final sum had appeared after what had seemed an appallingly arbitrary assessment of Will's income. It had abruptly halted an incipient slide into Conservatism when from an initial position of left of Tony Benn he had voted for a Tory neighbour in the last local elections who also happened to be on the town planning committee. A committee that would be soon asked to approve a planning application for an extension to Will's house. Will was clever. He liked money for what it could do for him.

Lewis half-smiled at Andrew. He remembered him from school. He was a couple of years younger than Lewis and he had known him as Will Watkins's son. Now he was a confident student willing to help them out on a Saturday morning, sure that he was doing them a favour.

They worked quickly. Talking amiably as they loaded the van with the stone which had only recently formed walls sheltering school children within stupefying lessons, insulated from the reality of the outside world: a world beyond the poster plaster walls and stunted syllabi; a world no one really knew anything about; beyond the textbooks, the stolen pens and desks smelling of dust and long-dried ink.

They were clearing part of the science block and Lewis could almost taste the endlessly repeated experiments of sodium and magnesium, sulphur and phosphate. The same experiments that had taunted him across numberless Tuesday afternoons; Marianne's smile engraved on a teacher's face.

'Why have they knocked this down then, Will?'

'Woodworm, the whole building was rotten with it.'

'How did you manage to get hold of the stone then?'

'I know the contractor. He's taking it all away Monday. That's why we're in today. I think it's being sold to Cadw to rebuild some farmhouse.'

'Did you get a good deal on it, Will?'

'C'mon, Roy, it's rotten stone,' revealed Will with a knowing smile.

The once imposing building was now a disorganised pile of rubble, miserable in defeat. The stones would have endured for another thousand years safe in their lithified death, but had been betrayed by the wood which had become infected by a dark rot that had swallowed its strength, forcing demolition.

Two foundation stones stood apart, slightly aloof from the common Pennant, the more expensive but more soluble limestone maintaining a respectable distance from the general mass. Etched but blurring into the limestone were the names of a long dead councillor and a retired colonel, patrons of the building. This had been their last final lunge for immortality in a tight forgotten industrial town. The names had been carved hoping for a passport into the future. A taste of permanence as Colonel D.L. Davies dreamed of the High Veldt and Evan Evans Bevan lamented a missed parliamentary nomination, while taking increasing consolation in his own brewery. The names are still there. You can read them yourself if you don't believe me but now they are commemorative bollards in a school car-park.

As they worked Lewis's hand began to swell as the fine black dust from the crumbling redundant cement infected his cut. With it the memory of another time seeped into his mind; his fist smashed across another man's face in front of Marianne. There would be no more chemistry lessons for Lewis, as there would be no more chemistry lessons, only rubble, for the scattered stones once forming the enclosing walls which he now laboriously hauled onto Roy's van.

The van could carry a ton and a half. They were able to fill it in ten minutes: Roy, Will and Lewis working hard, handling the stones easily; Andrew carefully selecting each stone, sizing it up before placing it gingerly on the van. Perhaps he had moved a third as much as the others.

'That's it for the load, Will; we'll tip this one at your house.'

'Right you are then.'

How much did you say you wanted?'

'Five ton.'

'Another two loads then. You boys wait here. And Lew, ask Mo Gwyn if he's going to work the next load or shall we drop him off in the park.'

Lewis and Will laughed easily. Roy smiled at Andrew. Andrew smiled vacantly back.

Lewis relaxed against the black school railings, allowing them to support his weight. Andrew shuffled uneasily around, for the first time in the morning unsure of himself. Lewis made no effort to speak, allowing Andrew to think of an opening.

'What did Roy mean about Mo Gwyn and the park?' asked Andrew, uncertain if he should have known the answer.

Lewis smiled before replying. 'Mo Gwyn is the statue in the park. Roy thought you were impersonating him.'

Andrew's face flushed in embarrassment but recovered quickly. 'Perhaps I should work a bit quicker next time.'

'The stones won't bite, you know, and they're all the same in the long run.'

Andrew smiled hopefully at Lewis, unsure how to react. Two girls passed the front gates of the school. Andrew waved before sauntering over to talk to them. Lewis watched his departure, content to be left to his thoughts. The school yard stood empty and the playing fields behind him were deserted except for a flock of black headed gulls feeding on an area of waterlogged grass beyond the roped off the cricket square. Soon the flags would begin going up for the morning's football matches. Football was the only game played on a Saturday morning since the demise of rugby; abandoned in a blaze of apathy. Neither game had interested Lewis in school; he had played because his friends were playing but the actual game had bored him, even frightened him. But since leaving school the club had absorbed increasing amounts of his time.

Across the schoolyard was the old art building, its fading

white paint flaking and fluttering to the yard from the rotting wood. Fading murals on the windows confirmed its purpose. Lewis had liked the building. He remembered the heat of the kilns on cold Wednesday mornings and the touch of paint drying his fingers. Falstaff had been the only teacher to believe him, but where was the influence of a fading middle-aged art master against the fiery self-importance of a young ambitious chemistry teacher? Falstaff had appreciated his loyalty in passing the art exam; the other teachers had ostracised him for it.

Andrew walked back up to Lewis as the van reappeared between the school gates, relieving Lewis of the need to talk to him further.

They resumed loading immediately. Stones resounded on the metal of the van's back as they tossed them on. Pain coursed through Lewis's hand as he gripped the stones again. The break had allowed it to become further infected. Andrew started work with a burst of frenzied activity, heaving stones like a deranged shot-putter high on amphetamines. Five minutes later he was breathing heavily, loading less than everyone else and his hand was smeared with blood from a hasty pick-up.

They quickly filled the van again.

'One more load then, boys.'

Roy and Will again departed with a loaded van, leaving Lewis and Andrew to wait. Andrew mooched around, his ego visibly deflating. He was not enjoying the morning. Lewis sensed he was about to make another attempt at conversation.

'You hoping for a win this afternoon?'

Despite the inanity of the question, Lewis answered. 'We've got to win this afternoon. Otherwise it's relegation.'

'Have you got a good side out?'

'It's not bad. We've had a few injuries through the season but I think it's more or less the strongest side now, but then Dunvant are strong and if they win they're assured of promotion.'

'They're having a good season then?'

'Yes, you could say that. Anyway, how's your hand?'

'Oh, it's nothing. One of the stones had a sharp edge, that's all.'

'I warned you they bite.'

Andrew smiled to hide his embarrassment. The morning was turning out to be more difficult than he had imagined.

'How's college going then, And?'

Andrew was relieved to receive a friendly overture from Lewis. He was also back on familiar ground.

'Great laugh. Pissed every night. Plenty of women.'

'You can do that here.' Lewis's voice suggested to Andrew that he was unlikely to be impressed by tales of drunken revelry.

'But here you have to get up in the mornings.'

Lewis grimly conceded the point.

'Some of the lectures are interesting, though. There's some sharp people there.'

'Hard work?'

'I've got eight lectures a week, one tutorial and an essay to complete every three,' announced Andrew conscientiously.

'Piece of piss, then?'

Andrew guessed that Lewis was unimpressed. 'It's not too strenuous,' he conceded.

'What do you do with your time, then?'

Andrew had a store of rehearsed answers for this question but was aware that Lewis was not going to fall for any of them.

'Lie in bed until about ten when I have to get up for lectures, watch tv in the afternoon and drink in the evening.'

Lewis gazed at Andrew through a thin veil of disgust.

'Good fun, then, is it?'

The return of Roy and Will relieved Andrew from answering.

'Right then, lads, last effort.'

They all began to load the van again. Several games of football had begun on the playing fields and their work was punctuated by a cacophony of shouts, cheers and whistles as the games followed their inevitable progress. The gulls, disturbed by the activity, huddled together in a far corner and sulked. More paint flaked from the old arts building, fluttering into scattered corners beneath the wooden frames. Lewis allowed another few hours to slip by in the ritual of work.

'That's it then, boys. Let's go.'

'A few more, Royston.'

'You don't need any more.'

'Might as well have them as we're here.'

'Give over. You've more than enough for that wall and my van has had enough.'

'Just these two,' replied Will as he bundled a further two stones onto the van. 'Meet you at the house then. Come up for tea, Lew.'

'I'm alright thanks, Will.'

'No, come up, mun. I can give you the money for the morning then.'

'Okay, Will. Thanks.'

Lewis climbed into the van alongside Roy.

'Nasty cut you picked up there. You didn't do it this morning, did you?'

'No, last night.'

'Fighting?'

'Well, not exactly. Jumping over a wall.'

'What were you wall jumping for?'

'Running away from the police.'

'What for?'

'Fighting.'

Roy paused with a wry smile before enquiring further. 'Did they catch you?'

'C'mon Roy. Do I look as if I've been in the cells all night?'

'It's getting hard to tell what you've been up to the night before.'

'No, they didn't catch me.'

'That woman's boyfriend didn't catch up with you, did he?'
'No.'
'Who was it over then?'
'Marianne.'
'She was home, was she?'
'Aye, and her boyfriend.'
'You didn't hit him, did you?'
'Afraid so.'
'Hard?'
'Hard enough.'
'Not exactly on talking terms with Marianne now, I take it?'
'I doubt it.'
'Never mind, there's always the girl at the building society.'

Lewis did not reply but dejectedly stared out of the window. No, he was probably not on the best of terms with Marianne now. She had not written for months, the boyfriend providing an unnecessary excuse. He hadn't seen her since Christmas and had not been with her since the summer. In significance her memory was fading to someone he'd once known even though he still chased her in his thoughts.

As they drove towards Will's, the spaces between the houses began to increase and after the road crossed a stream some people called a river, the houses briefly gave way to fields before larger houses claimed the land again. Will had moved here when his business had burgeoned. It was old land, lost by an absentee landlord who had accumulated Mayfair debts his country estate could no longer sustain. The peasants had eagerly moved in with their vulgar, recently acquired wealth: shopkeepers who had accumulated more than they had expected; solicitors in a second generation practice; mine owners and builders. They were all keen on being the lord of the manor, or if not the lord at least being in the right area to be on speaking terms with him. They had named their houses to mirror their aspirations: Manor Farm; The Old Gatehouse; Keeper's Lodge; The Cedars. They wanted the stability, the smell of permanence of an older, more ordered time that had lost its wealth in the chaos of two world wars. It was a prestige address.

'Nice area this, Roy,' commented Lewis as he attempted to peer past a screen of conifers to a pink house in the park beyond.

'Will likes it. Thinks he's moving up in the world.'

'He is, isn't he?'

'Which way's up? Don't lose your direction; you might find yourself somewhere you never intended to be.'

Lewis paused, considering Roy's builder's philosophy. It was a bit heavy for Saturday morning.

'Where's your direction? Where do you want to be?'

Lewis did not reply and Roy allowed the question to drop. He did not really want an answer. He had given Lewis a rough time on Friday. He knew when to leave him to his thoughts; there was too much of Lewis in Roy.

They pulled into Will's drive. He had already gone in. His house was a large mock-Tudor affair with a double garage.

'Let's 'ave a cup of tea then, Lew; I hope Martha's put the kettle on.'

Lewis followed Roy around the side of the house. I would imagine they sat at the kitchen table, talked about work and the afternoon's game, ate digestive biscuits, drank a second cup of tea and before they left Will handed Lewis two ten pound notes. It would pay for the night out in Swansea.

Roy drove Lewis home. It was gone twelve when he entered the kitchen. His mother stood over the ironing board removing creases from anything that had the temerity to acquire them. He sat at the table, automatically opening the paper that lay there. It would have been discarded by his father who would be now sitting in the front room awaiting the start of *Grandstand*. The house constantly absorbed a bombardment by the local radio station and an enthusiastic presenter announced its afternoon coverage which consisted of hyped sports reports. Lewis listened to nothing of the announcements. It was all background. His mother cut through his concentration.

'Good morning, love?'

Lewis looked up from the paper he was not reading and allowed the question to register before answering.

'Not too bad, Mam. Roy's brother was there and his son Andrew. It wasn't a hard job.'

'Andrew's home from college, is he? How's he getting on?'

There was a note of disappointed enthusiasm in her voice, which Lewis did not appreciate.

'Fabulous if you listen to him. Not much work in him though and he was giving us advice by the third load.'

'Ahh love 'im, helping his father out on a Saturday.'

Lewis didn't reply. The boy comes home from ten weeks of missing lectures, drinking and womanizing and he gets praise for helping his father out for two hours on a Saturday morning. Lewis attempted to submerge himself back into his paper but his mother was intent on talking.

'He's enjoying himself then?'

'Yes, I think so,' replied Lewis tersely.

Lewis was willing her not to make the obvious pronouncement, and she complied. 'An old friend of yours rang this morning. She wants you to ring her back.'

Lewis immediately gave his mother his full attention again. He tensely asked who it was.

'Marianne. I think she's home from college.'

'What did she say?' There was panic creeping into his voice.

'Nothing much. We had a little chat about things and she asked me to tell you that she'd rang.'

'Anything else?'

'You seem concerned. I thought it was all over between the two of you?'

'It is.'

'Well she seemed keen to talk to you.'

'I would guess she could be.'

'Why is that then, love?' asked his mother, sensing the possibility of something interesting.

'Nothing much, Mam. I bumped into her last night and she was with her boyfriend. We had what you might call a slight difference of opinion.'

'What did you do that for?'

'It just happened, Mam.'

'Lewis, love, when are you going to learn to leave her go? She's got a new life now.'

'I know, Mam. It just happened, that's all, okay?'

'Are you going to ring her?'

'Yes, probably.'

Lewis picked up the phone which was secured to the wall above the kitchen table. Usually he would have sought the privacy of the hallway but he just wanted the phone call to be over. His mother left to hang up the ironing.

He rang her number; it was etched in his mind. Three rings and her mother answered. There was recognition in her voice but it was cold and terse as if she was holding her feelings back. She promised to call Marianne.

'Hello.'

'Hello, Lewis.'

'Look, I'm sorry about last night. I didn't think.'

'Can I see you now?'

'Yeh sure, where?' Lewis looked at the clock above the kitchen door. He had to be at the club in an hour.

'Oswald's.'

'The café opposite the St. Ives?'

'Yes, ten minutes, Lewis.'

Lewis heard the phone being replaced before a cold tone

reverberated down through his receiver. Her voice faded slowly from his mind.

Oswald's was a glorified fish and chip shop off the square. They had met there regularly on cold Saturday mornings: hiding from the wind and the rain, waiting for the end of her lunch break, willing it to be longer. She had worked as a till assistant in Boots, a Saturday job, to subsidise her growing clothes bill. Lewis could still see the shape of her legs stretching the stiff white crimpline dress she wore.

'Mam, where's my kit?'

'In the airing cupboard love.'

Lewis hastily packed his kit and drove into town. He would drive straight from Oswald's to the club. Would she be there? Was it a trap for her boyfriend to meet up with him again? He was being ridiculous but he was nervous. He had wished for a chance to talk to Marianne for a year now; explain things; tell her it wasn't her fault; he hadn't meant his vicious accusations.

Sitting in Oswald's, faced by the fading rings of fading conversations, Lewis had finished his tea before Marianne arrived.

The sight of her clarified his thoughts. He realised why he was sitting in a small town café waiting for a girl who had left him and the town long ago. Why he had hit one man unprovoked except for a few drunken words and why he had hit another, five years before but not hard enough across a school table. He knew why he was still working his mind into putty during the day and drinking it to oblivion in the night.

'Hi'ah, Lewis.'

'Hello, Mar. How are you?' Lewis winced at the banality of it all.

'I'm fine, Lewis, you don't look too well. Your hair's short and you've let your face grow long.'

Lewis smiled. She was always better at quotations than him.

'You haven't brought your boyfriend along with you then? I imagine he's pretty keen to see me.'

'Don't mock, Lewis.'

'I'm sorry, Mar, I'm just nervous, that's all.'

'He's gone home. He wouldn't even speak to me,' Marianne revealed resignedly.

Lewis allowed her to offer an explanation but, as she didn't appear to want to, he enquired further. 'Why's that then? You didn't hit him as well, did you?'

Marianne shot him a glance that warned they were not yet back on the terms he was playing at.

'He was arrested, wasn't he?'

Lewis suppressed a smile. 'They didn't charge him did they?' he asked, hoping they had.

'Of course they did. He was in the cells all night. His father had to come and pick him up this morning. Warned him to stay away from his little Welsh tart.'

Marianne sulked into her coffee.

'Where is he? I'll hit him as well.'

'It's not funny, Lewis,' but she couldn't suppress a smile.

'What the hell did he do? He was out of it when I left.'

'Apparently he hit a policeman who was picking him off the floor.'

'Christ, what did he do that for?'

'I don't know. He was drunk, I suppose, like you,' she snapped crossly.

'I wasn't drunk.'

'That makes it worse. Why did you hit him, Lewis?'

'He was asking for it.'

'Oh, fuck off.'

'I've said I'm sorry. I didn't mean to hit him, well not exactly anyway.'

'What do you mean, you hit him by mistake? Grow up Lewis, when are you going to stop playing the fucking hero?'

'When you stop giving me reason to.'

'Don't talk crap, I never needed your help, not last night, not that time with Marshall either.'

'Fuck you then,' Lewis exploded.

Marianne stared at Lewis before replying calmly.

'Thanks, Lewis, that was very nice. Are you sure you don't want to hit me as well?'

'Look, I'm sorry, I'm just nervous, that's all.'

'It's no use talking to you now, Lewis. You're just a small-time boy, you haven't got it. You'll never leave this place or give up the job you hate so much.'

'Perhaps I don't want to, Mar. Perhaps it was always you who wanted to leave.'

'Well I'm leaving now. Goodbye, Lewis. You probably won't see me again. I'm away for the summer and then I'll be working. Enjoy your life and what you make of it.'

Marianne burst out of the café. Lewis looked around into the eyes of the gazing grannies and offended shoppers.

'What the hell are you lot looking at?' he challenged angrily.

'Aye, sonny get out and don't bring your tart back here again.'

'Why don't you fuck off, fatso?'

The fat fryer bulged his way out from behind the counter but Lewis had already gone. He didn't really want to fight a fifteen-stone lump of lard before the match.

He was still in the café as his volkswagen spluttered up the hill to the club. Meirion, one of the club's most committed drinkers, stepped into the privet hedge to avoid him as he spilled around the final sharp bend. He drew up on the red asphalt. Several players had already arrived, their cars standing vacantly in the park, collecting the light drizzle which promised to make the day difficult for handling.

Arthur, the groundsman stumbled out of the changing rooms' entrance with an armful of flags to mark the pitch perimeter. He would have already been out for an hour earlier, remarking the lines with white-lime in order for the game to be contained and to reduce arguments about feet in touch to an acceptable level. Arthur liked to think that he had been the groundsman for as long as anyone could remember, perhaps from before the war. But in reality he had taken it up after the railway had offered him a disability pension. He gathered a living between the pension, a small social security benefit and a sub off the club for the groundwork. It paid for his council house rent in the village, weekends of moderate but steady drinking and a few flushes on the horses, but only the big races: the Gold Cup, the Derby, the National and the one in France he could never remember the name of. He was not a great groundsman but then he had never intended to be. It was not a great ground. Built on the remnants of a coal-mine, it collected water like a rabid sponge. Grass avoided it and the mud had a congealing quality that had sucked the enthusiasm out of more than a few visiting teams.

Today the ground was not looking its best. The mud was bare and pools of water were scattered at random around the pitch as if left by a retreating tide.

'Afternoon, Arth.'

Arthur looked up from his feet.

'Hello, Lew, big game today, son. Looking forward to it?'

'It'll be hard,' replied Lewis, surprised by Arthur's enthusiasm. Lewis was still far from the game and would remain so until the first heavy knock warned him that it would be better to concentrate.

The club was quiet as he entered it but an air of expectancy clung to the walls, saturating everything. It was a scene he had known for what now seemed a lifetime: the pre-match smell of lingering beer wiped from tables with damp mats; of expectant pumps and kit bags; of stilted conversations and suppressed disappointments; of poolballs and video screens; grandstand and teamsheets.

The large outer room, used for discos and Christmas parties was deserted except for kit bags; it led through to the bar where most of the players gathered before the match to await the call to the dressing room.

Lewis greeted Joe with a smile, acknowledged several people whose names were not far enough to the front of his tongue to produce with confidence and sat down next to Alfie.

'Hi'ah, Lew.'

'Alright, Alf, who are you with today?'

'Seconds, Lew, up at Cwm-Flyn-Fech.'

'Nice trip, Alf.'

'Can't wait. Always a friendly up there.'

There had never been a friendly in Cwm-Flyn-Fech; the local hill tribesmen took it as a ceremonial rite to repel the invaders from the valleys with as much ferocity as they could muster.

'Mike was here a minute ago, Lew. Told us you were in a bit of a punch up in town last night.'

'Yes, there was what you might call a small disturbance, Alf.'

'No marks on you though, Lew.'

Lewis showed him his hand.

'Just a scratch.'

Mike appeared in the bar from the pool room where he had lost miserably.

'Hi'ah, Mike. Did you get away alright after?'

'You, you bastard, could have got us both nicked last night.' Mike was only half-joking. Then he laughed. 'What the fuck did you hit that bloke for?'

Lewis shrugged his shoulders, unsure how to respond. There were a hundred different reasons for hitting the boyfriend.

'You got away, didn't you?' enquired Lewis.

'Yes, I ran up the alley into the churchyard. They didn't chase me anyway; it was you that they were after. How did you lose them?'

'Into the castle grounds and up the river bank. They didn't get near me. They had him though; apparently he was banged up all night for hitting a policeman.'

'Christ, it wasn't a good night for him. Probably his first

night in town, gets beaten up, then locked up.'

'Par for the course really,' commented Alfie. All three of them laughed.

'Ah well, another night tonight boys. Are the seconds lads coming, Alfie?'

'Yes, we'll be down. What time is the bus leaving?'

'I'm not sure. Buzz is organising it. Seven, I think.'

'I'll ask him; he should be here by now.'

The club had swollen with an influx of players for the three teams and early supporters having a couple of pints before the game. The youth and seconds were away, the first team guaranteeing a home crowd of around eighty people and a few dogs.

'Ready then, lads,' announced Glenda from the pinnacle of a bar stool where he had been sitting shuffling team sheets with the secretary and seconds team captain. Glenda became his nickname after someone had suggested he looked like Glenda Jackson in a Ken Russell film or perhaps it may have been because he had once pulled a bird on tour called Zelda. Anyway the name stuck and in a curious way it suited him.

Glenda led the way through the changing rooms from the bar. Several players were already there in various stages of undress awaiting the arrival of the kit.

'They here yet, Glenda?' asked a voice, referring to the opposition.

'Yes, they're here.'

There was a tension in the room, a dull resonating tension that spoke of impending defeat, tired resignation at the end of an unsuccessful season.

Lewis noticed many of the faces who had missed training on Thursday night but he had ceased to care. Liniment singed his nostrils as his team-mates applied various forms of embrocation. Bandages and knee supports, head bands and ankle straps. It was a hard game but some people always over-did it.

The idle nervous chatter of the first few minutes faded into the self-stimulating exhortations to "Get your mind on the game, boys." Lewis allowed it all to pass over him: the team talks, the move explanations, the gentle and not so gentle encouragement. Sounds from the visitors' changing room filtered through and infected the atmosphere, souring thoughts and reminding wandering minds why they huddled together, changing in a cramped sweaty room with fourteen other men on a Saturday afternoon.

A tall figure in a purple jersey entered the room with a self-explanatory "Check your studs, boys."

He moved from foot to foot examining the length, form and roundness of each player's studs. He was more careful than most referees who usually only ran their hands along the bottom of each boot. Instead he examined each pair by eye and even asked one player to change two before warning another of their impending illegality.

He departed, announcing, "Five minutes then, boys."

Lewis still watched and listened without seeing or hearing anything.

'C'mon in one minute, Lew.'

Lewis joined a huddle of forwards.

'Right then, boys, sit down,' requested Glenda. Most of the team sat down although Daz still struggled to administer his various bandages, supports and dressings which were individually tailored to enable him to survive a game.

Glenda was about to embark on his perambulatory team talk when Dai Fats lumbered out of the changing room reminding everyone as he departed not to forget what he had told them on Thursday night. Lewis looked at his boots willing it to be all over.

Glenda tried again. 'We all know what we've got to do, and we haven't done it this season yet. This is our last chance to do it, or that's it, it's all over and we won't be doing it next season either. You all know you haven't done it. Daz, you haven't done it. Lewis, neither have you, Mike, Buzz, you haven't done it; I haven't done it. But we all know we're going to do it this afternoon because if we don't do it they'll do it to us, because they've been doing it all season. And Lewis, you watch the scrum-half. Right then, a quick one to ten and we're out.'

Lewis stood up to embark on what was collectively known as a psyche up. The reverberations of the opposition's warm-up invaded their minds as they embarked on theirs. It involved running on the spot, knees pumping high, while shouting the numbers between one and ten in an aggressive manner. How this was supposed to prepare mind and soul for a rugby match was a debatable point. But Lewis enacted the same ritual every Saturday five minutes before kick-off, occasionally he even enjoyed it. He watched the glazed eyes and listened to the shouted numbers while maintaining an acceptable level of participation lest somebody accuse him of not taking the whole thing seriously.

'Right then, boys,' shouted Glenda at the finale of the psyche up. He then led the fourteen players out of the changing room, images of Roman gladiators, Christians, lions and Charlton Heston filling his mind as he ran through the polite clapping of interested spectators who fringed the short route to the field.

Lewis ambled out of the changing room near the back of the column of players which followed Glenda onto the pitch. He kept his eyes on the player in front of him, feeling the hard concrete beneath his studs turn to soft mud as he accelerated onto the field.

The pitch was completely fringed by spectators. Dunvant had brought a busload, eager in their anticipation of clinching the league title over a bunch of relegation regulars. The Dunvant supporters fringed the near side of the touch line, outnumbering the smaller home contingent who slunk surreptitiously to the far side and huddled together under an elongated tin shed which served as a cover from the wind. The rain still threatened, hiding malevolently in the hills, waiting to sweep down the valley like a marauding raider.

Lewis turned to watch Dunvant run out. They seemed to burst forth from their changing room in expectation of a victorious afternoon. Somehow they looked fitter than the home side; taller, with tanned muscular thighs but Lewis was not concentrating and his active mind was exaggerating.

Glenda called his team to the far side of the pitch. He was going to play with the wind during the first half, hopefully scoring a few points which would act as a buffer, enabling them to hang onto the lead with the slope and the support of the home crowd in the second half. Lewis guessed it was a forlorn hope but it was probably the best option. Even with the wind they were going to have problems getting the ball over the try line. They were going to have problems getting the ball.

The match started with a high hanging ball into the forwards from the Dunvant outside half. Buzz managed to get his hands to it but knocked it backwards. Maddocks scrambled away the uncontrolled ball. The first half then unfolded into a kicking contest between Glenda and Dunvant's fullback. Glenda punted any ball that came near to him high into the air, allowing the wind to carry it to Dunvant, the forwards following and hopefully scavenging trys from any mistakes that Dunvant made. Unfortunately, Glenda did not allow enough for the strength of the wind which swept the ball too far upfield, enabling the fullback to gather the ball under no pressure and kick it comfortably to touch, where, from the line-outs their forwards would regain it before driving upfield through a succession of short bursts, rucks and mauls. Eventually their progress would be impeded by a knock forward or a loose ball which would allow Glenda to regain the ball and punt it downfield to start the process again. The home team were in a constant state of defence, tackling and kicking to keep their line intact. Lewis considered they were doing well in preventing a score, when five minutes before half-time after a succession of rucks, Dunvant's heavily built scrum-half forced his way over near the corner flag. Lewis watched him score from an excellent position. Their fullback missed the wide-angled conversion, making the half time score a respectable four nil. The game had already gone. As Lewis sucked his half-time orange and listened to Glenda demand more effort he realised the plan had not worked and it was time for plan B.

As they lined up for the second half amid shouts of encouragement from their supporters, Lewis recognised Dai Cwm huddled in his greatcoat, standing apart from the main crowd. He smiled at him, his mind still far from the game.

Five minutes from the restart after the Dunvant fly-half had successively kicked the ball high into the air to aid his forwards, they again crossed the line, this time near to the posts. A simple conversion made the deficit ten points. The home supporters, stretched along the far touchline already sensed the inevitable conclusion. Even among the mindless one-eyed optimists there was a note of despondency in their support, reduced to an occasional cliché of encouragement and mandatory disparagement of the referee.

Despite the wind and Dunvant's burgeoning confidence, the threatened rush of points did not materialise. They missed a few chances through over-elaboration as they became increasingly casual in their success. The home side, faced by their impending relegation, clung to the last vestiges of pride in a long season and tackled harder. Dunvant scored once more to take the score to fourteen nil and the game fizzled out into stuttering passing movements, inconclusive scrums and aimless touch-kicking.

A shrill double blast of the whistle pierced the March afternoon which was rapidly drawing a curtain over the day.

Lewis was on the floor, having just made a tackle. As he pressed his hands into the firm mud and congratulated the nearest opposition player he realised it was not just another match that had ended. A couple more friendlies and the club tour and that would be it for another season. He was uncertain if he would be playing come September. His enthusiasm was slipping away with the light of the Saturday afternoon.

The Dunvant players were quick to form a tunnel and clap their vanquished opponents off the pitch and into a lower division. Their enthusiasm was infectious to all but the committed. The thrill of promotion focused the whole season, justified the long wet training nights in mid-November and the frozen grounds of February. For Lewis it all appeared pointless. The rationale had become submerged in the mud and mistaken aspirations of his mind.

The changing room was overflowing with a silence punctuated only by the popping of champagne corks from the adjoining room. One of the committee commiserated with himself as he collected the jerseys; Glenda sat staring at his boots, flicking imaginary pieces of mud from them. Lewis drank a cup of heavily sugared tea, oblivious to the steam rising into his face.

He finally forced himself into the showers, where he shared a trickle of water with the opposition's fullback. The fullback offered him some shampoo which he accepted gratefully. They talked inanities, each wishing the other would finish so he could have the shower to himself. Lewis finished first.

Silence still dominated the changing room. Buzz shattered it.

'Could be worse, boys. We could all be getting married next weekend.'

There was a ripple of laughter, even from Mike. They all began to lighten up. At least there was a night out in the offing.

Lewis began to change into his suit which he had protected with a plastic coverall. In order to get into any decent club you needed a suit.

The bar was crowded as he entered it, the Dunvant supporters having already begun a night of celebration. The noise and fervour of victory saturated the atmosphere. Several regulars commiserated with Lewis as he made his way to the pumps.

'Fancy a round, Lew?'

Daz was standing at the bar.

'Yes, go on then, Daz.'

'What do you want?'

'Bitter, please.'

Soon two pints appeared hovering over the crowded bar.

'In the lounge, Daz?'

'Aye, let's get a seat. I'm knackered.'

They negotiated their way through a throng of people into the lounge. They were able to find a seat and half a table near the door. The other half was being used by two attractive but definitely married girls, presumably wives of the other team's players as neither Lewis or Daz recognised them.

Lewis smiled broadly as they sat down. The girls smiled a little nervously, a little contemptuously back as they sipped their Martinis and lemonade.

'Did you enjoy the game, girls?'

They were obviously surprised that Lewis had the temerity to speak to them.

'It wasn't bad,' replied the blonde one before giggling nervously.

'Your team played well.'

'Yes, they're good, see.' She could have added, "Unlike you," but politeness prevented it.

Lewis abandoned the conversation. Daz concurred with him and they sipped their beer in silence. It would take two or three pints to loosen up. There was food available but Lewis did not usually eat after a game. Daz returned with a plate of faggots and peas. The peas bobbed around the faggots in a calm sea of glutinous gravy. It did nothing to incite his appetite. He bought another two pints. They continued to drink in a sporadic silence punctuated by odd throwaway comments and interruptions from wandering committee men.

They were on their third pint before they started to talk consistently if not lucidly. Buzz had joined them. No one really wanted to discuss the game but it was a ritual that was impossible to ignore. Perhaps they would be able to expunge it from the collective memory. It had gone, been played and would be hopefully soon forgotten. Daz steered the conversation towards the evening.

'What time is the bus picking us up, Buzz?'

'It's supposed to be here at seven-thirty but knowing J.D. Jones that could be any time from about now until nine.'

''Ave you anything planned for, Mike?' enquired Lewis.

'Yep, I've got a strip-o-gram arranged; she's meeting us at Lucinda's.'

'Is she any good?' asked Daz eagerly.

'How do I know? John Windows booked her for me; he said he had contacts.'

'Aye, but what's she like? Is she, you know?'

'I don't know, Daz. I mean she probably takes her clothes off if that's what you're worried about.'

'That John Windows has contacts in everything. No wonder he's driving around in that BMW.'

John Windows was a centre for the seconds whose main business interest was replacement windows. His other contacts were unusually eclectic as any conversation with him soon revealed. He could get you anything from a cut-price pair of boots to a package tour in the Algarve. What he had arranged for Mike was anyone's guess.

'Where is Mike, anyway?'

'He's just popped home to change and apologise to Melissa. He'll be here soon.'

'What's he apologising to Melissa for?'

'Anything he might get up to tonight.'

'Never.'

'He is.'

'She'll probably be waiting for him at his mother's house, just to make sure.'

Mike arrived as they disparaged his prospective wife. He was resplendent in a new suit that he had bought especially for his honeymoon.

'Bloody hell. It's the man from C&A.'

'Burtons window nineteen-fifty-four.'

'Leave it out, boys; it's a good suit,' Mike responded, feigning offence.

'Are they marrying you or burying you, Mike? That'll make a great funeral suit.'

Mike enjoyed the comments. He would have been concerned if they had not ridiculed his suit as there would have definitely been something wrong with it then.

'Pint, Mike?' Buzz was the first to offer. Mike would have a cheap night as there would be plenty of boys keen to buy him a drink. He was a popular lad among both the players and the supporters of the club. The bus would be full on the trip to Swansea.

'Fancy a game, boys?' enquired Daz hopefully.

'Calm down, Daz, we've got all night.'

'C'mon, a quick game now before the rest of the boys arrive.' insisted Daz.

'What do you want to play?' asked Lewis.

'Well there's four of us so we could play Tip It.'

'Go on then, one round,' conceded Mike.

Tip It was a drinking game based on the correct position of a two pence coin in a choice of four hands. A correct guess and the coin was transferred to the other team. Three incorrect guesses and the losers drank a forfeit of half a pint. It was spectacular in its success if you required inebriation quickly. Otherwise over a couple of hands it was fun.

'I'm sure they're using two coins,' complained Buzz as he made his third mistake, requiring Lewis and himself to swallow the forfeit.

'It's just that you're crap, Buzz,' retorted Lewis.

The game foundered on a lack of reciprocal interest, leaving Daz futiley suggesting an array of alternatives.

The pints continued to flow steadily as they were gradually joined by more players from the main bar and also Alfic and John Windows from the seconds.

'How did you do, John?'

'Lost.'

'How much?'

'Twenty-six ten.'

'Where's the rest of the boys?'

'Scalped. Me and Alfie had to fight our way out, back to back.' John paused for the smiles before continuing. 'Do you want a pint, Mike?'

'Thanks, John, I'll have a bitter.'

Everyone drank, trying to ignore the singing that drifted in from the other bar. Dunvant were world-famous for their singing or so they claimed. Conversations rumbled along well worn paths: past matches and old stag-nights; marriage. Matrimony hung ominously over the beer-swelled congregation, oppressive in its pallor. Buzz reflected on his recent union, making it sound like the death of joy. Lewis hoped for a more enthusiastic response from one of the older boys but there were no dissenting voices. Daz listened to it all rapaciously.

'You take sex,' insisted Foster. 'For the first few months you can't get enough of it. Every night it's there waiting for you, no more living room floors or the back seat of a car. You've got your own bed, plenty of space, loads of time and no chance of an angry mother-in-law catching you. It's great, bonking all the time but then the routine bites in; there's no innovation or thrill of the unknown. It's regular sex, a quick jump, roll over and go to sleep. Sometimes you're pretending to be asleep to avoid it.'

The older lads laughed in concurrence with Foster. Lewis

laughed but felt a surge of abhorrence; it would not be like that for him. Now he could think of nothing more he wanted than time alone with the girl he loved. Nobody to hide from. It would be different for him.

Between them they slaughtered the sacred cow of marriage. It was fat and overfed; the meat would be poor.

'The bus is 'ere, boys,' someone shouted from the door. The time absorbed in the alcohol had become swallowed by many consummate appetites.

'Drink up then, boys. I'll collect the money on the bus,' announced Buzz.

Lewis was surprised by the latent organisational ability suddenly flowering in Buzz. Perhaps he was hoping another marriage would help him forget the immediacy of his own.

J.D. Jones was the coach company the club used for its away matches. It was neither fast nor efficient and a positive advert for re-regulation. But it was cheap. J.D. was a local legend. Perhaps everyone with initials instead of a first name becomes a minor icon. The advert on the side of the coach proudly proclaimed J.D.'s Continental Coaches: the continental proviso enthusiastically added after the Mecca bingo club had chartered a day trip to Calais. He was nothing if not an opportunist.

As Lewis climbed onto the coach, J.D. himself was sprawled over the driver's seat. He was a known drinker and it was Saturday night. Lewis should have been worried but it was a stag-night and drunken bus drivers were mere trivialities.

Lola the club choir master had already cornered the front seat from where he would lead the singing. Lola had a song repertoire founded in the 'sixties that was unparalleled by the most advanced Karaoke machine. Lewis was convinced he made a hobby of memorising obscure song-sheets in his spare time. He warmed up with a simple number from the Drifters.

A cloud of dust rose to greet Lewis as he sat down. He casually brushed the excess off. Daz sat down next to him.

There had been a big turn-out for Mike's stag-night and the bus was full. Suits that hadn't seen the inside of a nightclub since they were called dance halls had been prised from wardrobes before being pressed by bemused housewives and finally squeezed onto frames that had burgeoned beyond memory's desire to recall slimmer and fitter days. Mike stumbled on just before the bus was about to leave. If he had been any longer they would have probably gone without him. He was given a seat of honour next to Lola. Someone would soon suggest that he lead a song and Mike would be forced to decline in embarrassment. The singing swelled into a cheer as J.D. finally ground the bus into gear on its tuneless journey to Swansea.

'Good turn out, Lew. Most of the club have made the effort.' Daz was buoyant, 'I tell you what; I've seen some suits in my time but have you seen that thing Parks is wearing? I swear it must have been his demob suit.' He had obviously regained some of his enthusiasm for the evening. 'I'll tell you another thing,' continued Daz, 'Mike won't have another gathering this big until they're burying the bugger at the Crem.'

'That's a cheerful thought, Daz.'

'You know me, Lew; always look on the bright side of life,' he smiled as he sang the last line. 'Ay, remember Eric Idle singing that in the *Life of Brian*? Great film that.'

'Aye, I remember, only he wasn't as tuneful as you, Daz.'

'Cheers Lew.' Daz sang another verse before he continued cheerfully. 'Anyway, one's the same as the other, marriage is death if you ask me; you heard the boys deride it.'

'There wasn't that many good words for it, no, but I'm sure it must have a few redeeming points, otherwise everybody wouldn't do it, would they?'

'C'mon, Lew, look at this lot here tonight, out to get away from the wife for a night. Some of them wouldn't even recognise Mike. One old codger asked me if I was looking forward to the wedding; told him I couldn't wait for the free beer, which threw him slightly, so I just mentioned I was looking forward to the honeymoon and he toddled off pleased as hell.'

'I'll admit Swansea's the main attraction.'

'Swansea or the beer; they'll all be pissed as farts by eleven anyway.'

'Why do you think everyone has to drink on a night out then, Daz? Even us, we'll blow twenty quid tonight easy, wake up in the morning with a stinking hangover, remember half the night and convince ourselves we had a great time with the other half.'

'I don't know about you, Lew, but I drink to get pissed. If I didn't get drunk there wouldn't be much point, plus it's a laugh. I know you get the odd bastard who claims he can have a great time drinking three cokes and a Britvic orange but that's why he's drinking them in the first place: because no bugger will drink with him as he's so boring. It's a laugh; it loosens you up so you can forget about last week and try to keep next week out of your mind.'

'There must be more to it than that, Daz, something else.'

'Perhaps we're all closet alcoholics, Lew; it's no secret that it's addictive. There's just enough chemicals to keep us coming back. Anyway, I wouldn't worry about it too much, you'll be dead in sixty years and I bet you won't have a send-off like this.'

Daz liked his own humour; Lewis envied his ambience of unconcern.

The bus dropped down the valley before reaching a rendez-vous with the coast road into Swansea. The wide sweep of the bay was illuminated by a crescent of road lights to the west and the malevolent glow of the steelworks to the east. An optimist in the Welsh tourist board had once honoured it with the title, 'Naples of the North': unbelievably the comparison had found its way into the local folklore along with the pool where King Arthur lost his horse. Whether the bay of Naples is fringed by a steelworks and an estate of oil storage tanks is unclear. Perhaps it is, I've never been there.

The bus followed the road as it followed the bay, until it was swallowed by the expanding city in a rash of industrial estates, railway sidings and cheap terraces.

'Where are we going first then, Daz?'

'Lucinda's. Windows knows the landlord apparently; that's where the strip-o-gram is meeting us.'

'What, all of us?'

'If she's what I've been told, we can all 'ave a go.'

'Never.'

'Wait and see.'

Lucinda's was on the far side of the city, hiding on the corner of a road filled with Chinese takeaways, video shops and cheap hotels. The bus staggered up outside with Lola finishing his theme tune. There was a desperate rush for relief. The journey would not have been more than twenty minutes but the beer was not named piss water for nothing.

Lewis looked dubiously at Lucinda's: or Luindas if you read the neon sign. It had been masquerading as a wine bar but was now cheerfully freefalling down market after being forced to abandon its bourgeois pretensions out of financial necessity. This raid by a pissed stag-night would finally push it over the edge.

Lewis pushed himself into the instantly full one-room bar. The barmaid had panicked hopelessly in a rush of orders she would not have expected until ten-thirty if at all. The landlord had forgotten to mention his agreement with Windows or to provide any extra staff.

The room was dark, with a green tinge to the light provided by the plastic pot plants which smothered the bulbs. It made the clientele, already seedy, look positively ill. The owner had once been to Greece on a package tour and had enthusiastically modelled the bar on 'a little taverna' he had discovered 'off the beaten track' on Mikonos. This had resulted in an interesting marriage of styles as earthenware pots competed with décor land prints and cedar tables stood upon a beer-saturated carpet.

'Ere you are, Lew.' Daz was never slow in procuring drinks. Getting served in a crowded bar was a knack. You either had it or you didn't. Lewis had tried to improve his technique for years: striking dramatic poses, standing on his toes, juggling money. All to no avail. He was hopeless; but Daz was a natural.

The taste of alcohol again after a thirty-minute break was consoling. It forced Lewis to consider the addictive powers guessed at by Daz. You didn't need to look far for proof. Town was littered with drunks, some more spectacular than others. All small towns had their pensionable drunk; it was niche employment at its most specialised. There was one local drunk; everyone knew him. People called him a character as if it conferred some source of excuse, absolved people of their sins, a sort of respectability in removing the dirt of the reality, lest it happen to them. His name was Geoffrey, never Geoff, always Geoffrey. He could be found sleeping in the park by day and wandering the town at night. When it was confirmed that Geoffrey had died on one of his periodic visits to hospital in Cardiff the whole town had known in a matter of days. There had been a trust fund set up to erect a memorial, a permanent commemoration to remind people of their faults lest their soul be similarly blackened. The fund foundered on a technicality when several days later the ghost appeared, pissed but definitely alive, stumbling into the post office on a Thursday morning where it harangued the queue for a share of its collective pension. You see, Geoffrey had once been someone. He had talent: an artist who had once been at the Slade. One of his drawings hung ominously in the museum, illuminating what had once driven him. A mediocre sketch but there was an idea there: a will to achieve; to be recognised, a desire that had first been stimulated by the drink and then drowned. The failed artist drunken into submission in an attempt to rediscover or find a talent that may never have been there: the thought that haunts every drunk. Did he have talent or was he just a drunk? There are enough talentless drunks who need no excuse.

But the obvious did not stop Lewis drinking. It obstructs very few; even the religious drink. It's a release, a need to be absolved of sins you might commit. The night will always pass quicker with alcohol as a drinking partner and the night was flying.

There was a splinter of excitement within the bar as it became known that the stripper was about to arrive. Among hushed voices and hidden glances the party gradually sidled towards a door at the side of the shrubbery. John Windows led the way through to a seedy backroom which doubled as a kitchen. Mike was complaining to Buzz about the predictability of it all.

'I knew you'd get me a fucking strip-o-gram. Melissa will kill me if she finds out.'

'Oh, don't moan. It's only a bit of fun for the boys.'

'The boys. What about me? I've got to get married next week.'

'You don't count. It's only your stag-night, you could 'ave stayed in the house.'

Lewis sympathised with Mike but didn't say anything. Mike didn't know what he was in for yet but then neither did Buzz.

The room was packed. Everyone was in for the action. They clung to the walls, stood on chairs and sat on the sink. The centre of the room was left bare. It would be the stage.

Lewis stood behind Buzz.

'I hope you know what you're doing here, Buzz, I don't think Mike is going to like this at all.'

'Don't worry, Lew, it'll only be a bit of slap and tickle.'

'We'll see, Buzz.'

Buzz gave him a questioning look but Lewis decided not to elaborate any further. Perhaps Buzz was right.

A roar from the boys near the door heralded the arrival of the 'Sensualist'. It was a title dreamed up by her manager in one of his most benign moods. A stripper she was not, there was nothing on worth stripping in the first place. Thickly applied make-up attempted to hide the passing of more than four decades. Sagging flesh was everywhere, a red g-string hid her fanny but nothing more. Two pendulous bosoms swung freely as she wobbled into the room.

'What the fuck has Windows done to me?' yelped Buzz above the tumultuous roars.

The Sensualist plucked a young looking lad from the front row. To the accompaniment of baying laughter she dragged him into the centre before plunging him into her chest and then pushing him down to her crotch. The yells increased as he struggled before she threw him back to the pack.

Lewis could feel himself backing further into the wall as if it offered a chance of escape. He was intrigued and revolted by the spectacle. The boys he knew had turned into a buoyant baying mass howling for action: for excitement. A sexual excitement invisible but seen by all. There were a few uncommitted faces but most had become absorbed in one mass erection.

The Sensualist had now plucked another hound from the pack. Had he placed himself close to the front to attract attention? Lewis was unsure. There was something too eager in his acquiescence to having his balls rubbed in front of thirty spectators. She expertly pulled his dick out through his fly. It rose visibly in her hands as she gave it a few sharp tugs before she pushed him back to the obscurity of the crowd.

'Fucking hell, Lew, Mike is going to kill me,' bleated Buzz.

'Well she's not what one would call tasteful,' offered Daz.

'I did warn you, Buzz.'

'Bit fucking late.'

'With Windows, you pay your money, you get no choice, you know how it is.'

'I do now, Lew.'

'Did you see what she just did with that Newkie Brown bottle?' exclaimed Daz.

'Fucking hell, it didn't touch the sides.'

'She'll have Mike supping out of that now,' predicted Daz.

'Leave it out, boys, I'm in enough trouble already. What if Melissa finds out?'

Mike had attempted to back away from the centre of attraction but insistent, expectant hands had forced him back to the front. The Sensualist had known all along who her real target was; she had used the others as a warm-up. The baying crowd were now calling for blood, or if not blood at least a blow job.

She snaked her wobbly path towards Mike, who surveyed his fate with abject terror. Before he could resist he was pulled into a cleavage of classical proportions. The back of his head was just visible beneath the converging flesh, arms flailing ineffectively at his side.

'Aye, Buzz, she should be called the Anaconda not the Sensualist,' commented Daz. Buzz didn't reply.

The Sensualist removed Mike from her breasts. He gasped for air, his face crimson with a panic no longer simulated. Before he could react further she pushed his head into her now stringless fanny. The tension in the cheers intensified. Mike forced his head out of her grip but appeared to be unwilling to escape. Castigation would follow if he baled out.

She recommenced her improvised dance routine which involved getting as much of herself as close to Mike without actually swallowing him. The calls became fierce shouts of incitement as she positioned herself kneeling in front of Mike. Her hand rose and began to unzip his fly. Before she could get her hand on his dick he was gone. The potential humiliation suddenly paled, the willing shouts meaning nothing as he bolted for the door. Mike was leaving a pub in a hurry for the second night in succession. Disappointed arms attempted to restrain him as he ran for the door but the desire to escape was too strong: he took two tacklers with him as he stormed through. The room erupted in laughter as the tension escaped with Mike. The Sensualist re-adorned herself with her one item of clothing and a coat provided by her ever-present manager.

'Aye, Buzz, it's a pity Mike didn't run like that this afternoon. We might have won.'

Buzz remained silent but Daz offered a further note of complaint.

'Fuck, boys, I don't know why we're leaving. Her manager says she'll do an encore for thirty quid.'

Nobody took him up on the offer.

John Windows was waiting for them in the bar.

'What happened, boys? Mike just legged it out of here,' stated Windows.

'I think he was hoping for something a bit more up-market. You know, somebody with clothes on to take off.'

'Strip-o-gram you said, Buzz; you didn't specify.'

'I was hoping you would use some discretion. It's his wedding next week, after all.'

'She was good value for the lads, wasn't she?'

Buzz did not reply.

'Where were you anyway?' asked Lewis.

'Not my scene, lads, I've been in here drinking.'

'Who's doing the explaining to Mike, Buzz?'

'I expect I'll have to. Anyway let's get the fuck out of this place and find him.'

They found Mike two hundred yards up the road in the wrong direction for the nightclub. He was still genuinely scared but fortunately for Buzz embarrassment had soothed his anger.

'You fucking arsehole, Buzz. If I wanted a cheap tart I wouldn't be getting married next weekend.'

'Sorry, Mike, I honestly didn't know. John Windows did the booking.'

'Forget it, mun, Mike, you got away, didn't you?' suggested Lewis.

'Ay, Mike, you could still be in the arms of the Sensualist

back there. She would have crushed you by now,' predicted Daz helpfully.

Mike glared at Daz, then grinned as the tension drained from him.

Lewis collected the situation. 'Right then, boys, which night club is it? We might as well go in. What about Juliet's?'

'The Aviary is the best,' asserted Daz. 'The women are easier.'

'What about the Rank?' asked Buzz.

'Give over, Buzz, your grandmother will be in there.'

The city's lights called them and they walked. The noise of the city at night, slithering along radiating streets from its rotten core, sucking them in.

The centre had been bombed into a developer's dream during the first months of the real war; since then it had been arbitrarily erected, demolished, re-designed and re-erected again, leaving it disfigured into a dissonance of styles only architects admired. Tourists called it ugly and rushed on through to the Gower; locals, if pressed, would unassuredly insist it had character.

It was in this discordant centre that the city's night life had festered. Discos and bars cancerously swelling in old cinemas, supermarkets and bingo halls, spreading rapaciously along a stretch of the city known as the Kingsway. The police detested it, M.P.'s lamented it, the paper ran stories on it. It had a persona all of its own, a torpid malevolent lizard, and on Saturday night it stirred from its innocuous daylight slumber and bit anyone who crossed it.

The stagnight as a whole had dispersed into the Kingsway, swallowed, transmogrified, assimilated into the Way. Some would regroup later but many would be lost until the next stag-night enticed them out of their hollows. A night's pass only lasted until the day turned and the frog princes would become couch pumpkins again. Fast blacks offered an escape route.

The half-drunk foursome waited in the inevitable queue at the entrance to the Aviary. For Lewis the alcohol was beginning to steal his lucidity, spiriting the evening away. Time was losing its coherence, minutes were slipping into seconds and seconds into hours. Recent events were memories; current action began to have a blurred unreal edge, sometimes heightened, sometimes dulled.

The Way was a mass of people all in search of the ultimate Saturday night fix. The urban valleys had spewed out their youth for sacrifice in the city. Coaches bused them in pissed, allowed them to sate their desires or burn their frustrations for a few hours before carrying them back to a parental home, to cosseting and protection, killing time before exchange for another woman to cosset and protect.

Lewis watched it all in detachment with a veneer of disdain, knowing he was part of it, despising himself for being unable to see an alternative. There was the traditional escape but surely there was something else.

'Right, in you go, lads.'

The bouncer invited them into the birdcage. It took a second to adjust to the light. A wide staircase with mirrors on the walls and lights on the steps led to the dancing on the first floor. The Aviary was one of the smaller night clubs on the Way and apart from a predilection to a strong Swansea accent it was filled with an eclectic mixture of nightclubbers from thirty-year-old divorcees to lapsed students.

'Your round, Lew.'

Lewis made his way to the bar. It had only just gone eleven and the club was rapidly filling up. As the pubs closed, throwing out their drunken cargo, most would search for another three hours drinking time. A day's work would flow away into the tills of the landlords and breweries. The great

Saturday night gorge to blacken the soul, preparing it for another week of drudgery, of human time given for small remittance.

Lewis found Daz at the edge of the dance floor.

'Where's Buzz and Mike?'

'I think Buzz is at the bar. Mike's over with some of the lads from the club.'

'They've made it in, 'ave they?'

'Yes, a couple of them, how the bouncers let them I don't know.'

'How's that?'

'They're all half-cut.'

'Everybody in here is half-cut, Daz.'

Daz gulped a mouthful of his drink.

'Any good looking women in here, Lew?'

'Thousands, Daz.'

'Where?'

'Aye, sure.'

They both stared at the milling figures on the dance floor.

'Fancy dancing with anyone, Daz?'

'Yes, I fancy it, but I don't fancy asking.'

'C'mon, then, let's go.'

'Who with?'

'Those two over there will do.'

'You're joking.'

'C'mon.'

Daz would have backed down but Lewis was already striding purposefully onto the dance floor. The drink had infused Lewis with the necessary confidence. A pair of girls were dancing together near the centre of the floor. Lewis stepped to the side of one who surveyed him with practised indifference. Daz belatedly arrived to dance with her friend. Lewis allowed himself to gyrate with the music. It was only when he was drunk that the alcohol was sufficient to lubricate his dancing. To him it was a patently ludicrous activity, a mating ritual where you debased yourself with a series of movements arbitrarily co-ordinated with the rhythm of a song you probably didn't like or even know.

The end of the song extended itself into a series of re-mixed drumbeats and backing vocals. He was thoroughly bored by the time it eventually faded into the next song. The girl took the opportunity to smile facilely at Lewis before walking off the dance floor. Her friend followed her.

'What the fuck did you say, Lew?'

'Nothing, I don't suppose she liked my dancing style.'

'I'm not surprised, but I was in there. I was getting the right come on.'

'Fuck off.'

'Honestly, her name was Sarah and she was from the Mumbles and works in Debenhams as a cashier.'

'Fucking hell, Daz, you got her life story.'

'It was more than you got.'

'Look, Daz,' said Lewis smiling, 'I don't talk, I just dance.'

Daz laughed. They were back at the bar. The one rebuff was enough for Lewis. He concentrated on his drinking, determinedly chasing oblivion.

The beer was expensive but it had already been paid for. There was no comparing of prices now. It was drinking time. The club began to absorb Lewis into its alcohol-saturated atmosphere. Time was running to the money removed thoughts and forgotten actions. Daz drank to keep up but he couldn't concentrate.

'Lew, hold this a minute. That girl's over there, I'm going to talk to her.'

Daz disappeared into the crowd in search of the Debenhams check-out girl. He did not immediately return so Lewis drank his pint. He was then forced to buy another one. He had finished that when Daz arrived with two three quarters-full glasses.

'It's my round, Daz.'

'Don't worry, 'ave these, I just picked them off a table over there.'

Drink pinching was an acceptable and sometimes essential pastime in expensive night clubs. It was a cheap way to a drunken night followed by a terrible hangover. In the hands of an expert it became an elevated art form. The key was audacity and a convincing look of innocence if questioned.

Lewis finished his second free drink. Daz had presumably found the Debenhams girl. Nobody else had come up to talk to Lewis and he was past the point of making the effort himself. He smiled vacantly at a stream of passing faces who passed away into the darkness. The realisation that he was being supported by a mirrored pillar as he gazed onto the dance floor with only an empty pint glass to console him, forced the thought of leaving. He made for the exit, legs swimming with fluid, vision blurred through a crystal haze of Marianne.

The Way again confronted him as he winged his path out of the birdcage. Oblivious to its own vulgarity it sauntered menacingly, drawing people around, clothing itself in their garments and drunken thoughts. The police were outnumbered: they clung to the corners in the lee of their pure white vans, wary of the Way and its malicious intent. They hated it, but without a uniform it would draw them mercilessly into its nefarious habits. There was only one escape: babysitting.

A line of buses trailed into one of the side streets. Lewis was ready to find J.D. Jones. The night had gone.

'Lew, mun, are you deaf or what?'

'Uh? Oh alright, Buzz, no, didn't see you.'

'Coming for an Indian?'

'Don't know if I could manage it.'

'C'mon, the bus won't go for an hour yet.'

'An hour?' asked Lewis miserably.

'Aye, it's only one.'

Lewis didn't really want an Indian but he didn't really want to sit on the bus for an hour either.

'Hang on I'll see if I've got enough money.'

He checked his suit pocket which revealed a crumpled five-pound note and about a quid in change.

'Aye, okay, where're you going?'

'The Prince.'

'Where's that?'

'Don't worry, it's just down Marlybone Street.'

Lewis tagged along with Buzz and Mike who was unusually coherent for his own stag-night. The Sensualist had impaled him with a sobriety that would outlast the alcohol.

The Prince of India was a squalid takeaway which had expanded its business by apathetically converting a back room and tacking on an ill-conceived extension. The pink walls were stained brown at the corners with cigarette smoke, the occasional smudge a food stain. The carpet was similarly adorned.

'What the fuck are we doing here, Buzz?' enquired Mike.

'It's cheap and we probably wouldn't have got in anywhere else.'

'Bollocks.'

'It's not that bad.'

'It's worse.'

'It'll all taste the same this time of night anyway, Mike.'

'It'll taste a lot worse in the morning when it's coming back up, Buzz.'

'Stop moaning, it's alright 'ere, mun. I'n it, Lew?'

'Uh?'

'It's alright here?'

'It's okay,' replied Lewis unconvincingly.

'What's the matter, Lew? Too much to drink?'

'Just feeling a bit dazed, that's all, Mike.'

A waiter arrived. He begrudgingly took their order. There was contempt in his eyes. He hated his job: serving these ignorant inappreciative drunks. They couldn't even tell a biriyani from a masala. There had been too many insults and base racist jibes, too much faceless hatred, enmity and resentment; too much thrown food. It was only his family commitments which kept him working. If Lewis was sober he may have sympathised but tonight he merely stared at the table-cloth and gave his order.

The waiter left through a swing door directly into the kitchen. The brief glimpse of disorder should have deterred anyone, but who was looking?

The waiter returned for the money. Lewis handed over his crumpled fiver; Buzz contributed a handful of coins. You paid first or there was no food.

'Where are you going, Lew?' asked Mike.

'Bog.'

Lewis rose unsteadily to his feet. He was not sure which direction to move but followed another customer who appeared to know where he was going.

He pushed his way past a swinging plywood door into the back of the restaurant. A stylised picture of a man in a suit and tie identified the toilet. He waited for the other customer to finish. The man came out zipping up his fly. Lewis gratefully pushed past him into the single toilet. The smell of piss hung like a veil over the small cubicle. He peed vigorously but unsteadily over the bowl spraying the already saturated tile floor. He backed out not wishing to flush the chain. There was distaste but no nausea.

You can build up a level of resistance to men's toilets: some are better than others but they all have piss on the floor; fag butts and one pence coins in the urinals; the lock is always broken and there is never any toilet paper after nine o'clock.

The short corridor back into the restaurant confused him.

He pushed the door open only to find himself in a dimly lit room stacked with boxes and tins. He sat down on one of the boxes and hung his head in his hands. The night surrounded him. It had played with him all evening, daring him to go further, to chase oblivion and now it stealthily took its chance. He would not be fully awake again until the morning. Twenty minutes stumbled past Lewis as he sat in the storeroom of an abysmal Indian restaurant on Marlybone Street off the Kingsway. Sunday morning was waiting only a bus trip away. He forced himself out of the storeroom, blindly pushing a door open. He was out in an alleyway to the side of the Prince. He followed the glare of lights to the front. Forgetting about the food, he stumbled towards the Way and J.D. Jones. A route back or out.

After three attempts he found the correct bus. Several of the boys were already on. Someone greeted him as he climbed onto the steps. He did not reply as he slumped into the refuge of the first empty seat.

Sometime later the jolt of the bus pulling off roused him from a semi-sleep of tired dreams. The Way rushed past his eyes again. It had began to slither back to its lair: content to slumber away the daylight hours building up its malevolence in the factories and shop arcades until it stirred for another Saturday night.

SUNDAY

Sunday morning dragged its intrusive presence over Lewis's mind, forcing him to accept its inevitability. As long as he remained half-awake, allowing his thoughts to wander unhindered, the full reminder of Saturday night could not assert itself. But it waits and has eternal patience.

Real hangovers are not an abstract thought; they are not a concept; they have a reality. And by real hangovers I don't mean a small headache in the morning after a sweet sherry and a few glasses of white wine. A real hangover has a persona. It exists. It is there sitting inside, hovering, recounting. It resents you, punishes your every movement, taking salacious pleasure in its obvious effect. It has opinions and it knows why it exists: with malicious intent and self-righteous airs it asserts its own authority. Aware of its own strength, it will persist for a day, before it steals back, to sit in expectant relish of its next inevitable return.

A touch dramatic perhaps but why not read it on a morning when a hangover literally hangs over you?

Yes, I'm waiting now, waiting for it to descend. I can't move, but soon I will be forced to get up for a piss and then I'll have to continue with my story. I will have to tell you what happens: if you're still reading. You're still reading, aren't you?

It's been an uneasy relationship, Lewis and me. I don't know how we've kept together so long. How's it been with you?

I'm awake now and the hangover has subtly reminded me of its presence. So considerate. It will be around all day before it grudgingly fades into the background of Sunday night television. But now it has an opinion on everything I attempt to do or think.

As I endeavour to get up, its weight is oppressive. It hurtles from one side of my head to the other, forcing my skull outwards. It feels like it could break out but I know it will not. It doesn't want to.

The walk downstairs is tedious. My mother will be in the kitchen either ironing or cooking the lunch. I know this because she always is. The efficiency is frightening. Have I mentioned this before? She will have already been to church, praying for my salvation. I think she was waiting up for me last night. I wish she wouldn't; it can get embarrassing. She has stopped me pissing in her cupboards before now. I sleep bollock-naked and when I'm drunk I sleepwalk. The possible scenarios are frightening if I care to think about them. I suppose she is my mother and will have seen me naked before now. But.

'Morning, Mam.'

She doesn't answer. I must have been really drunk last night. I wonder what I did. The only thing I can do now is sit at the breakfast table and stare at it. Something will happen soon. My mother is casting various looks of displeasure to disgust from the high moral ground of her ironing board. I don't think she is going to say anything.

'What state do you think you were in last night? It's disgusting getting that way.'

Obviously I was wrong but she hasn't mentioned anything specific so perhaps I was just plain drunk. I'm not going to reply as it will only exacerbate the situation. But now she's started she's bound to continue.

'I hope you feel ashamed of yourself.'

For what? I ask myself, but not her.

166

'You're suffering now, good, it's self-inflicted injury. I've no sympathy for you.'

I know that, Mam, I just wish you could leave my hangover and me in peace so that we can enjoy the morning. We're getting on famously. I'm not daring to respond as I'm in no state for an argument. She'll hopefully stop in a minute. It's boring running a one-sided row. You've got to be really committed to enjoy it.

'I'll tell you another thing: if your father had seen you in that state there'd been hell to play.'

C'mon, Mam, you can do better than that old cliché. She's tiring now. Her enthusiasm is visibly draining. The way she is folding that ironing is a lesson in precision point making. I'm not interested.

She is finally leaving the kitchen. I'm not sure if she thinks there's a moral victory somewhere. Maybe there is but I've missed it.

Breakfast now seems an appealing prospect but I have to concentrate hard to open the fridge. There's half a pint of milk waiting for me which I gulp down. There's no taste at all. The alcohol absorbs more than your mind.

I now try the cupboard in search of cornflakes. There is an unopened box which throws me for a while but I eventually succeed in obtaining a bowlful.

It is strange how an idea can lose its appeal so quickly. The cornflakes are now absorbing the milk, marooning themselves as if abandoned by the tide. The first spoonful tastes of nothing, so I give up.

Through all this the hangover is in constant attendance: still waiting, still malevolent and very vindictive. It will probably reach its zenith around twelve. For the next two hours it will be in the ascendancy. Christ, you could make a fortune selling pills to cure hangovers. Some people do. Nothing works. I tried taking vitamin pills for a while: it was supposed to 'arrest the deanimation of amino acids in the brain, the loss of which causes hangovers'. Well that's what the advertising said anyway. They turned my piss green but the hangover was still there, laughing at my attempt to remove it. Anyway, I digress. I must get back to the story.

I'm waiting for the phone to ring. It will because I'm waiting for it to ring. And the next couple of lines will record that it has rung. It's like that in stories: you can make things happen. Nothing really matters. Nothing. In a hundred years the mind that is reading this will be dead, will no longer exist. There will be a few fading photographs, a bundle of penned words fading in an attic drawer, more if you're famous, maybe only a film or two but don't get too excited as the chances are it will be a home video. But that's it unless of course you believe in an afterlife, a heaven perhaps?

Marianne will ring me this morning, about now probably. She will need to talk to me and we will arrange to meet where the river crawls around the churchyard. She will want us to be together again. I will agree for that is what this book is all about: a reconciliation with someone I once knew as someone who knew me; a time I left before she left me. All the inferences are simply that; you can make what you will out of them. That's up to you.

The phone is ringing. I said it is ringing so it is so.

'Hello, Lewis.'

She sounds determined. I wasn't expecting that. I was more prepared for a weeping woman. I am better with weeping women; it gives me an advantage, a feeling of power.

'Will you meet me?'

'Yes.'

'The churchyard, at twelve.'

See, I told you we would meet. Did you doubt me?

It was twenty to twelve before Lewis ventured from the breakfast table. He placed the half-eaten bowl of cornflakes in the sink hoping someone would wash it. That someone had retreated upstairs in protest at his drinking; the dinner had still not been started. His father would be hungry this afternoon.

It was a ten-minute walk to the churchyard, perhaps fifteen with a hangover. The hangover was still with him, insistently absorbing the morning. Thoughts of Marianne filtering through it.

Outside reminded him that there was life beyond his kitchen table. Sunday morning still existed. People drove to garden centres or carpet superstores, in-laws visited each other, a handful even went to church.

He cut through a lane towards the church. Bare trees swayed in a strong wind that had seared the pavements dry. White railings, gathering with rust, guarded one side of the footpath. Beyond them a waterlogged field, silver pools glistening as the wind rushed clouds past a peeping sun.

Who saw all this? No one. Lewis walked blankly ahead. A moment preceding the Spring that nobody saw. No one would recall.

The gates of the church loomed into his path. Its congregation was congregating, resplendent in their Sunday best. Everyone appeared old, even the young. Everyone eager for their Sunday lunchtime absolution.

Lewis watched them enter, leaving expensive cars in the carpark even while the church roof was being blown off. To the back of the car-park he recognised a figure as she picked her way through the graveyard, having followed the path around the river. She smiled across the distance.

He walked into the graveyard. It was closely manicured around the church but rapidly absorbed itself in overgrowth closer to the walls. He followed Marianne as she turned away to the river, catching her as she walked under the cover of a yew tree, its needles thick on the floor swallowing the weeds.

Without speaking they kissed. She held him, squeezing his arms, prolonging the touch. They both knew that they would never touch again. Time was forcing them apart. Forever intimates always on the periphery of someone else's seclusion.

The sound of the church organ drifted across the headstones as Lewis pushed Marianne back against a crypt. He read the inscription even as she curled her hands around his jeans.

A self-inflicted absence through too many mistakes made too early.

'What if there is no one for you, Lewis?'

Her words touched him as he felt the cold stone of the crypt. Hands grappling with buttons. Nowhere to go but inside.

There was no more talking, only the drift of voices from the choir behind the stained-glass window that shielded the congregation from a sacrifice beneath a cross that was never theirs to witness. Beneath a crucifix, on a slab of hewn pennant, under a knotted yew, they cursed their love into a lost cameo frozen with memory.

As his body comes inside hers so briefly joined before release, no one will witness the burning of dreams while semen glistens in globules on yew needles surrounding the memory of Arthur Raymond who lies beneath.